# HYDRA: A GREEK ISLAND TOWN

# HYDRA: A GREEK ISLAND TOWN

## ITS GROWTH AND FORM

## CONSTANTINE E. MICHAELIDES

PUBLISHED FOR WASHINGTON UNIVERSITY BY

THE UNIVERSITY OF CHICAGO PRESS, CHICAGO AND LONDON

*Library of Congress Catalog Card Number 66-20584*
The University of Chicago Press, Chicago and London
The University of Toronto Press, Toronto 5, Canada
© *1967 by Washington University*
*All rights reserved*
*Published 1967*
*Printed in the United States of America*

ΤΟΥ ΠΑΤΕΡΑ ΜΟΥ ΚΑΙ ΤΗΣ ΜΑΡΙΑΣ

Detail from a nineteenth-century painting by G. Drivas (the complete painting is reproduced on page 21). The town of Hydra is shown in the background in a schematic but still recognizable form. Note the predominant volumes of *archontica*, windmills, and the characteristic features of the topography of the site. Courtesy Historic Archives of Hydra.

# FOREWORD

Artists and critics are concerned about what seems to be the disassociation of art and life in the modern world. Forms to which artists react are often too esoteric for the lay vision. And the environment produced by the everyday building process seems to artists to be incredibly banal and ugly. So such powerful plastic ideas as the Roosevelt Memorial are rejected by both the Roosevelt family and the Congress, while "America the Beautiful" is described by its more charitable critics as "God's Own Junkyard."

It is therefore reassuring that both architects and the lay public find evocative certain man-made environments of the past: New England villages, Hopi pueblos, Italian hill towns. The town of Hydra is such a place. The town and its natural setting have both the unity that is characteristic of all art and the diversity of any environment that provides a rich life for its inhabitants.

Architects and laymen, for different reasons, reject, at least at the present moment, the notion that we can recreate Hydra in the American suburbs. But we still should be curious to understand the nature of the forms we respond to so unanimously and to analyze the building process that produced such forms.

This study describes a handsome town in a handsome way. It may also suggest lessons for a world sorely in need of help in shaping its environment.

Joseph R. Passonneau

*Washington University*
*St. Louis, Missouri*

7

# PREFACE

The strong character of the architecture of Hydra impressed me during my early visits to the island, but it was after an extensive absence from Greece, when I had a new opportunity to visit the town during the summer of 1960, that I started thinking of Hydra in terms which eventually produced the present study. At that time it occurred to me that the architectural character of the town was not so much the outcome of certain isolated "happy events" as much as it was the consequence of an over-all form—an impressive, perceptible, and consistent form. Two nineteenth-century visitors have registered this impressiveness very well:

"Hydra itself is a barren rock. But on turning the eastern points on the principal harbor, the town opens like an enchantment. It is the only town in the island, contains nearly 13,000 native inhabitants, and the white houses, thickly set and out-topping one another as they ascend from the water high up the rocky hill, are together an exhibition of surprising beauty. A nearer view increases the traveller's surprise—at the dimensions of the houses, their structure, their furniture, their elegance."[1]

"Enter its little harbour, and cast your eye upward, and you are astonished and delighted at the amphitheatrical spectacle of snowwhite dwellings, rising in succession above one another, from the water's edge up towards the crest of the rock. When gazing on this rock-built city in the stillness of the evening, it appeared to me one of the most striking objects on which my eye ever rested."[2]

The form of the town is "perceptible" in the sense that it can be associated with the simple shape of a classical theater. But beyond this, the form delineates clearly where the town starts, where it ends, and where its center is; and it provides the visitor at every instance with the physical means of orienting himself within the context of the city. Finally, the form of the town is "consistent" because its structuring concept is present in every detail and every possible scale.

This form was attained within a relatively recent historical period which was of short duration. The peak of Hydra's development occurred in a forty-one-year period between 1774 and 1815 when, by odd historical circumstance, this small and unknown island of the Aegean Sea found itself riding the high waves of contemporary European events.

[1] Rufus Anderson, *Observations upon the Peloponnesos and Greek Islands Made in 1829* (Boston, 1830), pp. 143–44.

[2] Reverend John Hartley, *Researches in Greece and the Levant* (London, 1831), p. 169.

View of nineteenth-century Hydra reproduced from William Linton, *The Scenery of Greece and Its Islands* (London, 1842). It seems to me that this lithograph has been printed in reverse. Courtesy Cleveland Public Library.

Because of its prominence then, the island's history is reasonably well documented.

This study is an attempt to analyze the form of Hydra and to place it in its proper context, in the hope that the process will enrich our understanding of how and why cities grow, what cities are, and what they are made of.

I am greatly indebted to the American Institute of Architects—American Institute of Architects Foundation Scholarship Program and to Washington University for the financial support which enabled me to spend the summer of 1963 on Hydra, observing the life of the town and collecting the data and material on which the study is based.

I am also indebted to Dean Joseph R. Passonneau for his continuous interest and much needed encouragement throughout the study, and to Professor Sam B. Warner of Washington University for reading the manuscript and making enlightening suggestions. In many respects the idea for this study was the outcome of my association with Professor Eduard F. Sekler of Harvard University, to whom I also feel indebted.

9

View of nineteenth-century Hydra reproduced from
Henri Belle, *Trois Années en Grèce* (Paris, 1881).

My thanks go as well to the people of Hydra for their warm reception of someone measuring their homes, and, in particular, to the personnel of the Hydra City Hall and Hydra Archives for making their facilities available to me. I should also like to thank Mr. Antonis N. Manikis, editor of the review "To Mellon tis Hydras," for the information he provided me about the history of some of the town's prominent family houses.

Dimitris Antonakakis, a Greek architect, kindly allowed me to refer to the measured drawings of his study of Hydra's streets. These drawings facilitated the task of data collection on the site. Students from both the University of Thessaloniki and Washington University helped in the collection of data and their transformation into meaningful drawings.

My last and profuse thanks go to Miss Myrl Funk and Mrs. Mildred Scott for their patience and care in typing the manuscript many times over.

C. E. M.

*Washington University*
*St. Louis, Missouri*

# CONTENTS

# PART I
# HISTORICAL BACKGROUND

North shore of Hydra.

## GENERAL INFORMATION

When, in the 1850's, Queen Amalia of Greece asked an Hydriot about the products of his small island east of Peloponnesos, he answered that "the island produces prickly pears in abundance, splendid sea captains, and excellent Prime Ministers," describing laconically and accurately both the natural conditions on the island and its exceptional contribution to contemporary Greek life.

The island of Hydra is a rocky, treeless ridge, about eleven miles long, two to four miles wide, and about four miles off the southeast coast of Argolis. The stony, precipitous hills, capped by two-thousand-foot-high Mount Ere, offer only four hundred acres of arable land on the island's dry, 18.5 square mile area.

According to legend, water used to be abundant on the now almost waterless island. Some have even attributed the name of the island to that fabled abundance. It may be that the frequent earthquakes, which still occur, were the cause of the transformation of Hydra, but its waterlessness is of long standing. In the past the Hydriots built numerous cisterns to collect rain water, and they still rely on them to meet the problem of water shortage. But even rain is scarce. The average yearly precipitation in the area during the last thirty years has been only an inch and one-half.

Hydra has a moderate climate with temperatures ranging from a high of 100° in the summer to 32° in December and January. In this climate the town of Hydra, the island's only large modern town, supported a population that was as high as twenty-eight thousand in the prosperous 1820's, but which had dropped to twenty-five hundred by 1961.

Since the town's small harbor is not well sheltered, during its prosperous years Hydra's naval yards were located at Mandraki, a small inlet to the east, connected with the town of Hydra by the island's only road. In 1844 the island was granted the privilege of sending three representatives to the National Parliament for one hundred years, in recognition of its exceptional contribution to the Greek War of Independence in the 1820's. Today Hydra is under the department of Attica and is the seat of the bishop of Hydra and Spetsai.

## EARLY YEARS

Until the Byzantine era there is little mention of Hydra in the well-documented history of Greece, a fact which indicates Hydra's sparsity of population and unimportance in affairs at that time. In these early days Hydra seems to have been a favorite temporary shelter for the Peloponnesians fleeing invaders from the north. The prolonged wars in the sixteenth and seventeenth centuries between the Turks and the Venetians contesting Peloponnesos, however, created the conditions for permanent settlement of the island.

While these settlers were by tradition shepherds and farmers, the poor soil of the island and the limited pasture

Characteristic Hydriot landscape.

land turned them to the sea, first as a source of food and later as an avenue for communication and commercial relations with the outside world. This transformation of shepherd and farmer to fisherman and sailor was gradual and took place over a number of generations. The first abortive attempt by an Hydriot to build a ship was made in the 1650's, but it was in the latter part of the century that Hydra's prominence in seafaring began, as a result of an incident which brought hardship and despair to many of the island's families.

A number of Hydriots had been taken prisoner by a raiding party of Algerian pirates and placed in forced labor in the Algerian shipyards. Here the prisoners acquired an

13

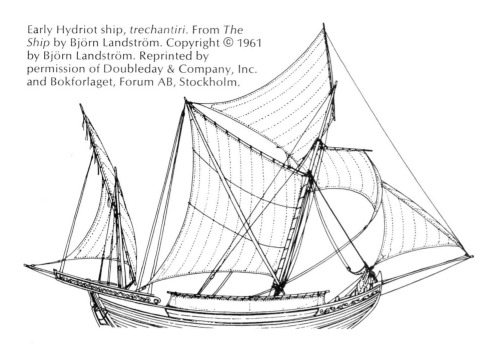

Early Hydriot ship, *trechantiri*. From *The Ship* by Björn Landström. Copyright © 1961 by Björn Landström. Reprinted by permission of Doubleday & Company, Inc. and Bokforlaget, Forum AB, Stockholm.

elementary knowledge of shipbuilding. After being ransomed and returned to Hydra they applied their new knowledge to the construction of Hydra's first ships—the *trechantiria*—a type common in the Mediterranean at the time. Small, with oars and three sails, the *trechantiria* were used to carry foodstuffs and wine for sale or barter to the neighboring islands of the Aegean Sea.

After 1715, when the last Venetian strongholds in Peloponnesos surrendered to the Turks, Venetian sea power in the area declined and Hydra's commerce expanded rapidly. Soon new ships, ranging from ten to fifty tons capacity, extended the travels of the Hydriots. The coast of Asia Minor, Smyrna, Constantinople, Crete, were now within reach. Venice came next, and in the 1750's an Hydriot captain brought back from

this port the island's first compasses and maps. These instruments enabled the Hydriot ships to travel to every corner of the Mediterranean, and some of the more venturesome passed through Gibraltar and reached the Americas.

## THE EIGHTEENTH CENTURY

There were other factors which led to the emergence of Hydra's merchant marine beside the island's limited natural resources and the courage with which the islanders took on the sea. By the middle of the eighteenth century Hydra, despite its small size, found itself playing an important part in the internal life of the Ottoman Empire, and found itself affected, though less directly, by some of the most important events of late eighteenth-century European history.

*Hydra's Special Treatment by the Turks*
Between the capture of Constantinople by the Ottoman Turks in 1453 and the Greek War of Independence in the 1820's, the history of the lands enclosing the Aegean Sea was highlighted by a succession of wars and revolts. Hydra's colonization was initiated by these wars, but its subsequent and substantial development owed more to the acts of mutual accommodation and co-operation between the Greeks and the Turks.

After the final Turkish conquest of the Venetian possessions in southern Greece in 1715, Hydra, with the rest of the Aegean Islands, was placed under the command of the Great

14

Map of "Graecia" by Johann and Cornelius Blau (1638–40) showing "Sidra."
Courtesy Map Division, The Library of Congress.

Admiral of the Fleet and under Turkish taxation laws. Turkish taxes were of four categories: head tax, tax on pasture land, tax on agricultural products, and customs tax. These taxes were rather light for Hydra because the island, together with a number of other Aegean islands, was subject to another form of taxation: the annual contribution and maintenance (which included food, clothing, and salary) of a number of young islanders as recruits for the Turkish fleet. This form of taxation allowed the Turks, a people without a seagoing tradition, to maintain their control over the vital sea routes of their empire by transforming the Aegean Islands into recruiting grounds for the Ottoman fleet.

The relationship between the Turkish authority and Hydra was a continuous game in which each side tried to use the other to its own advantage. On one occasion in the 1770's, the Sultan signed a decree granting Hydra the privilege of collecting its own taxes as a reward for losses suffered by Hydriot crews in the Turkish service. The independence from Turkish administration and control which this decree afforded was important for the future development of the island. At times the Turks, pressured by the Hydriots, mediated and secured the release of ships caught by Algerian pirates; they also permitted the Hydriots to arm their ships to protect themselves against the numerous pirates of various nationalities. But the Sultan, correctly anticipating the events of the Greek Revolution, limited the tonnage of ships built by Hydriots, lest their size and number become a real threat to the Ottoman power.

*The Appearance of Russia in the Near Eastern Scene and the Treaty of Kutschuk-Kainardji (July, 1774)*
Russia's emergence as a major European power during the eighteenth century was immediately felt in the eastern Mediterranean. Hydra was affected both because of its geographical location and because of its political, national, and religious structure.

Early in the eighteenth century the Russians realized that their elevation to the status of a major European power depended mainly on their ability to expand their trade through the Black Sea to the Mediterranean. The Turks, who at the time controlled the Black Sea and egress to the Mediterranean, were the obvious obstacle to such an expansion. The Russians also thought of themselves as the rightful heirs to the Byzantine Empire, and as the champions of Slavs and Christians under Turkish domination. As an economically emerging nation they looked for ways to realize their goals of expansion.

Peter the Great was the first Russian ruler to orient his external policy toward these goals. By the reign of Catherine II (1729–96) the north shore of the Black Sea had finally come under Russian control, but unrestricted access to the Mediterranean had not been attained.

Catherine II also realized the important role the Christian subjects of the Ottoman Empire, particularly the Greeks, could play in implementing her policy of expansion in southeast Europe. The Greeks, too, had come to realize that in their attempts to shake off Ottoman rule they could not count on substantial help from the West. Greatly impressed by the Russian achievements and by Russia's emergence as a major European power, and encouraged by their religious affinity, they turned their hopes and expectations toward St. Petersburg.

A minor incident in 1768 brought Russia and Turkey to war—a war long planned for by both sides, which lasted about six years. During this war the Russian fleet of the Baltic Sea sailed around Western Europe and made its appearance for the first time in Mediterranean waters. At the sight of the fleet, most of the small islands of the Archipelago revolted against Ottoman rule and were taken over and occupied by the Russians for a number of years. Russian successes on both sea and land resulted in the conclusion of the war by the Treaty of Kutschuk-Kainardji, signed in 1774.

According to the treaty, areas occupied during the war by the Russians were restored to the Turks on the specific promise of better treatment for the local population. In general, Turkey recognized the right of Russia to interfere—if necessary—in Turkey's internal affairs on behalf of her Christian subjects. Furthermore, Russia established a permanent foothold on the north shore of the Black Sea, secured the right of free navigation in that sea, and maintained the right of free passage for her merchant ships to and from the Black Sea and the Aegean.

The provisions of the treaty of Kutschuk-Kainardji were supplemented in 1783 by a commercial convention according to which the islanders of the Aegean obtained the tremendously important privilege of sailing and trading under the Russian flag and under the protection of the Tsar. This protection afforded the islanders immunity from any kind of Turkish interference. It seems, from the great number of illustrations of Hydriot ships shown flying the Russian flag, that the islanders realized the value of the privilege and took full advantage of it.

*Conditions in the Mediterranean During the Latter Half of the Eighteenth Century and the Napoleonic Wars*
The rapid rise of Hydra's merchant fleet was also due to the decline and in some instances the complete disappearance of other flags from Mediterranean waters.

When Diaz rounded the Cape of Good Hope in 1486, a serious and eventually fatal blow was dealt to the naval and commercial power of Venice. Venetian possessions in the eastern Mediterranean were lost one by one to the Turks, and the republic's importance as a naval power constantly diminished, allowing, particularly during the eighteenth

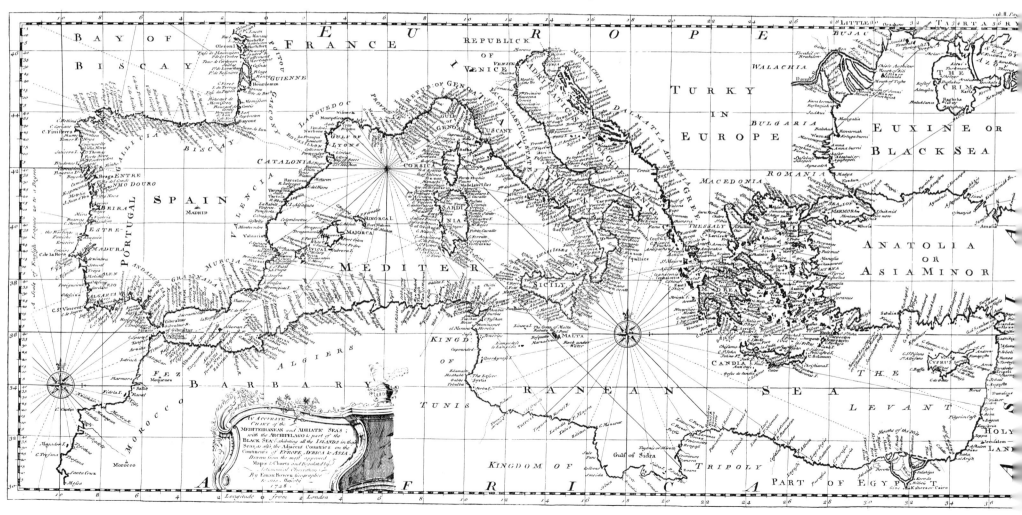

"An accurate chart of the Mediterranean and Adriatic Seas; with the Archipelago & part of the Black Sea exhibiting all the islands in those seas, as also the adjacent countries on the continents of Europe, Africa & Asia . . . 1748," by E. Bowen. The map shows "Sidra I." Courtesy Map Division, The Library of Congress.

century, for the expansion of Hydra's navy. The invasion of northern Italy by Napoleon, and the Treaty of Campo Formio in 1797, which concluded this campaign, ended the existence of Venice as a power.

The French merchant marine played an important role in Mediterranean commerce during the eighteenth century. But the French Revolution and its subsequent events weakened that importance. Here, as in the case of Venice, much of the commerce previously conducted by the French fell to the Hydriots.

The great opportunity for the island occurred later, however, during the Napoleonic Wars. By breaking the English blockade of French and French-controlled ports, Hydriot captains amassed sizable fortunes. Figures from the archives of the island show an average yearly profit per ship, between 1810 and 1815, of 80 to 100 per cent on invested capital. Immediately after the termination of the wars, profits went down sharply both in percentage of invested capital and in terms of actual sums of money.

Running the blockade was a highly profitable undertaking, but it also involved great risks. Hydriot ships were often captured and confiscated. The archives of Hydra contain correspondence pertaining to the capture of several Hydriot ships by the English. One letter is addressed to the admiral of the Turkish fleet asking his mediation for the release of a particular vessel. However, a letter was also addressed directly to Nelson, regarding the same ship, thus illustrating the degree of autonomy enjoyed by Hydra and the level of self-confidence attained by the islanders. A number of other documents from the Hydra archives indicate that Hydriot ships were built specifically to run the blockade, with speed as the most important design consideration.

In summary, tremendous opportunities were opened up for Hydra by a combination of events: Russia's conquest of the north shore of the Black Sea, particularly of the areas between the great rivers, brought the wheat of the Ukraine to the seashore. The Treaty of Kutschuk-Kainardji and subsequent agreements permitted Hydriot ships to raise the Russian flag, rendering both the ships and their owners immune to any kind of Turkish interference or persecution. The treaty also opened the Straits of Bosporus, the Dardanelles, and the Sea of Marmara to the free passage of merchant ships under the Russian flag, which now included most of the ships of Hydra. Since other merchant marine were unable for various reasons to take advantage of these "open seas," the transportation of wheat from the granaries of the Ukraine to the western Mediterranean ports fell to the Hydriots. And finally, the Napoleonic Wars and the English blockade provided a rare opportunity for large profits for the daring islanders.

19

# THE MERCHANT FLEET

From the sometimes fragmentary tax reports and lists of ships in Hydra's archives, one can draw a reasonably accurate picture of the size and composition of her navy. Between 1786 and 1806 Hydra had from 86 to 158 ships. The largest ship owned by the island in 1806, the first year actual tonnage was recorded, was 451 tons. In 1815 there were 23 ships listed with tonnage over 400 tons. By comparison, it is interesting to note that the *Endeavour*, the ship Captain Cook used for his first voyage to Australia and New Zealand in 1768–71, was 370 tons with a crew of 34.

In 1757 the first large ship (250 tons) was built by Hydriots in Corinthia because of the abundant timber supply there. In 1787 the island's first brig was built in Fiume, and by the late 1790's the *trechantiria*, *sakturia*, and *latinadika* were almost completely replaced. The 1812 list contains 106 three-masted barks and two-masted brigs, and only 27 schooners.

The extent of the travels of the islanders determined the size and form of their ships. As long as they sailed primarily in the Aegean the traditional lateen sail remained the predominant form-giving element; but when their travels extended beyond the local waters to western ports, bigger western-type ships were introduced and adapted to Hydra's particular needs. Foreign-made ships were sometimes bought by Hydriot captains at various ports such as Genoa, Fiume, or Marseilles.

The Turkish Great Admiral allowed the ships to be armed with cannon for protection against pirates. The Hydriots, however, relied mainly on speed and maneuverability rather than heavy armament. Cannon meant a reduction in the ship's cargo. Illustrations show that early ships were armed with as few as two cannon and that bigger ships of the late eighteenth and early nineteenth century carried between ten and thirty cannon. Ten to fourteen men were needed to man a small ship, while seventy to seventy-five manned the largest Hydriot ship.

Hydra's ships were at first hired as transports at nearby commercial centers. As the economic power of the island grew, the ownership of both ship and cargo came into Hydriot hands and was organized in a co-operative manner unique to a few Greek communities of the late eighteenth century. A voyage was a joint venture of shipowner, captain, and crew. None were salaried; each shared in the profits or losses of the voyage. The capital for the cargo purchases was provided partially by the shipowner or local merchants, the rest by the captain and the crew. According to the Maritime Law of 1804, the rates of interest to be paid for the

*Athiná,* brig of Captain Tsamados, painted by G. Drivas in 1871. Oil on canvas.
Courtesy Historic Archives of Hydra.

The three-masted bark in the center flies the revolutionary flag of Hydra. Other Hydriot ships at the corners fly the Russian striped flag. Oil on canvas. Courtesy Historic Archives of Hydra.

Profit sharing was first established by custom and in 1804 codified by civil law. The clear profit of the voyage was divided in the following way: half went to the shipowners, and from the other half the captain took three parts, the senior crew members two or one and one-half parts each, and crew members one part each. Often one part was given to the island's monastery or used for some other communal purpose. The act of sharing the profits always took place at a meeting in the captain's house on the Sunday or holiday immediately following the return of the ship. In many cases the shipowner and captain were the same person, although by common practice ship ownership was divided among a number of persons so that loss of the ship to either rough seas or pirates would be more easily absorbed.

capital needed for the purchase of cargo were defined according to the distance covered in the voyage from Hydra, rather than according to the time of the investment. For example, the rates for Malta or Sicily were 15 per cent, for Naples 17.5 per cent, for Genoa 20 per cent, for Barcelona 25 per cent, and so forth. Captain and crew drew interest from this investment in addition to sharing the final profit of the voyage.[1]

[1] It was rather surprising to me to find so many similarities between Hydriot practices and those of the New England communities discussed by Samuel Eliot Morison in his *Maritime History of Massachusetts, 1783–1860* (Boston: Houghton Mifflin Company, 1941). One example of this is voyage financing. Similarities can also be found in the very origins of the two communities. Morison says of the New Englanders: "Stark necessity made seamen of would-be planters." "Massachusetts went to sea, then, not of choice, but of necessity." (Pp. 11, 12.)

## HYDRA'S GOVERNMENT

During the early years of Hydra's development, and up to the middle of the eighteenth century, the Orthodox clergy, as the "educated" people of the time, played a very important role in the government of the island in addition to their religious duties. However, in the later part of the eighteenth century, as more and more of the islanders, through their travels in Western European lands, came into contact with progressive ideas of government, and as

Three-masted bark of Hydra, painted at the end of the nineteenth century. Oil on canvas. Courtesy Historic Archives of Hydra.

certain families with interests in the affairs of the community became prominent, the government of the island fell into the hands of laymen.

Antonis Miaoulis, historian of the island and son of Admiral Andreas Miaoulis, who was commander of Hydra's revolutionary fleet in the 1820's, says that Hydriots were divided into three groups. The first group was made up of the heads of the wealthy and prominent families; the second group was composed of the sea captains; and the third, of the people (*demos*), which included all sailors and artisans. While the strongest voice belonged to the first group,[2] the opinions of the captains were invited and respected. The third group did not directly participate in governing the island, but no decision was made without their consent.

The government of Hydra during the later part of the eighteenth century was oligarchic-representative. A body of qualified representatives—primarily composed of members from the first group—elected a number of its own members to perform the functions of government for a limited time. Advanced age and wealth, as well as achievement on the seas, were the necessary qualifications for participation in government. The election of the governing representatives took place in common assembly of all qualified members. Generally six to twelve representatives were elected to serve for one year, with rotation every month. They normally dealt with the day to day affairs of the community, the compilation of annual tax lists, the enforcement of public safety laws, the keeping of the communal finances, and so forth. On important occasions, in response to demands from the Great Admiral of the Fleet for new recruits or requests for special contributions, for example, all representatives would assemble to decide on proper action.

Hydra's autonomous status was also reflected in her direct relations with the western powers, particularly those

[2] Morison again says of seaboard Massachusetts: "Few town meetings have been held near tidewater where the voice of shipowner, merchant, or master mariner did not carry more weight than that of fisherman, counting-room clerk, or common seaman." (*Ibid.*, p. 23.)

23

Hydriot sailor, from Henri Belle, *Trois Années en Grèce* (Paris, 1881).

powers with which the island had extensive commercial transactions. Foreign consulates were established on the island to facilitate these transactions and to protect the interests of foreign ships and subjects. The earliest consul (French) was mentioned in 1782. A Russian consulate was established before the end of the eighteenth century. Later, England, Austria, and the Ionian Republic were represented by consuls.

Around the turn of the eighteenth century the old oligarchic system seemed no longer able to command the loyalties of the people. Again, liberal ideas introduced from abroad by the sailors were probably the main cause. These ideas found expression in acts of individual violence, however, rather than in any organized political activity. Sailors often refused to comply with the traditional ways of voyage profit sharing when they were not favored by them. Also, order became difficult to maintain because most captains now flying the Russian flag and paying Russian taxes would not consider themselves bound to the island's Turkish-appointed government.

A protracted period of public disturbances led the heads of the prominent families to appeal to the Turkish Great Admiral for the appointment of a strong governor with extensive powers. They specifically requested that Captain George Voulgaris, an Hydriot serving in the Turkish navy, be sent for the post. Voulgaris was appointed by the Great Admiral as the first governor of Hydra at the end of 1802.

Voulgaris' first act as governor was to select ten representatives as his advisers and to create a civic guard through which he restored order. Then, to avoid further disturbances, old customs of oral business dealing were transformed into precise laws as the Maritime Law of Hydra of 1804, the Customs Law of 1809, the Tax Law for Ships and Commercial Buildings of 1810, and so forth.

The most challenging event of Voulgaris' governorship took place in 1807, as a consequence of a new war between Russia and Turkey. Again, a Russian fleet, this time under

Admiral Siniavin, appeared in the Aegean. But this time the situation was different from that of 1770. Most of Hydra's ships were now under Russian flag, and Siniavin simply commanded the subjects of the Tsar to support and supply him. The islanders had no alternative but to join Siniavin, and Voulgaris went into voluntary exile. A Russian officer took over the administration of the island in the name of the Tsar.

The Russian fleet withdrew before the end of 1807 after it had won two minor naval encounters with the Turks. Now Voulgaris had to exhaust his powers of persuasion to extract a pardon for his fellow islanders from the Turkish Great Admiral. The new sultan, Madmud II, granted amnesty for all those who had followed Siniavin, thus closing another turbulent chapter in Hydra's history. Voulgaris died in 1812 and was succeeded in the governorship by Captain Kokovilas, who remained in this position till the eve of the Revolution in 1821. During Kokovilas' governorship the codification and improvement of rules of public transaction continued. The Civil and Maritime Law of May, 1818, and the Customs Law of December, 1820, were enacted, and numerous price control ordinances were issued.

## CHURCH AND EDUCATION

Immediately after the conquest of Constantinople in 1453, Mohammed, the Turkish sultan, conferred on the Greek Patriarch, and consequently on the Orthodox clergy under him, considerable civil as well as religious authority over the Christian inhabitants of the empire. This double authority of the Church worked to the advantage of both Greeks and Turks and served as one of the strongest formative factors of life for the Greek community during the years of Turkish domination.

Archbishops and bishops were empowered to hold civil courts to resolve matters of inheritance, family differences, and all other civil problems within the Orthodox community. This practice was particularly favored by the Greek population since Turkish justice meant exposure of their personal holdings and wealth to the Turkish authorities, which in turn invited blackmail or confiscation. The Church, then, was involved in one way or another in every facet of life in the Greek community, making itself an indispensable part of tradition and culture.

The islanders, by tradition, were very religious people. Often exposed to the perils of the sea, they found comfort in, and entrusted their safe delivery from danger to, holy intervention and the saints of the Church. The many small churches and chapels which are found in all the islands of the Archipelago were votive offerings from sailors expressing their gratitude to the various saints to whom they appealed for protection. Hydra is full of such churches (more than one hundred) within and beyond the limits of the town.

Originally, Hydra came under the jurisdiction of the archbishop of Aegina, an island to the north. But her increasing

Four Hydriot churches. These are small "one room" chapels which usually belong to a family. Note the characteristic whitewashing of walls, and the indications of outside influence in the stone volutes of the bell towers.

population and economic potential resulted in the transfer of the archbishop's seat to Hydra itself in the 1770's. The number of parish churches in the town was much greater than its size would indicate. For example, in 1782 there were twenty-two; in 1820, thirty-eight; and in 1828, when the native population was sixteen thousand five hundred, there were fifty-five. This can be explained by the distinctive topography of the town site: a steep site makes the same distance harder to travel than on a level site, and the townspeople therefore built many churches to spare themselves much climbing. The large number of churches and the small number of parish-

ioners for each made the financial status of the parish priest unenviable. As a result, many priests occupied themselves with some other profession becoming to their religious stature.

During the years of Turkish domination, the Orthodox Church also provided, through its clergy, for the education of the Greek people. Public, secular education was unknown to the Turks, but religious education was both practiced by them and permitted to their Christian subjects. Hydra was no exception. The education of its young people was exclusively in the hands of the clergy until the middle of the eighteenth century. Reading from and writing about the Acts of the Apostles, King David's Psalms, and finally the Gospel summed up the cycle of formal Hydriot education of that time. Contacts with the outside world changed this situation, and in 1749 the first school with a teacher hired by the community was opened on the island. The teacher was, nevertheless, a person with religious affiliations —a monk or a priest whose only duty on the island was to teach its young. A contract between such a teacher and the community, dated 1816, has been preserved in the archives. Besides stating salary and fringe benefits (the teacher was to get a sum of money plus fifteen kilos of wheat, fifty kilos of cheese, and a certain amount of olive oil), it defined the subjects to be taught: grammar, logic, metaphysics, rhetoric, moral philosophy, geometry, physics, Italian, and Bible reading every Saturday.

At an early age, Hydriot boys were taken on the ships where they performed usual chores and learned their future profession. They thus acquired an empirical knowledge of sailing, but their formal education was considered important as well. A naval school for the island's future captains already existed in the 1780's with Italian and Portuguese teachers. The islanders' concern with education was also indicated by the fact that the community repeatedly paid the expenses of Hydriots studying abroad in fields other than those dealing with the sea, such as medicine and education.

## DECLINE

The peak of Hydra's prosperity occurred around 1815. With the end of the Napoleonic Wars and the resumption of normal life in Europe, other merchant marine (French and English, for example) began to recover their prewar position in Mediterranean commerce. The island now had to compete with strong adversaries and saw difficult times, with many of its ships moored and its sailors unemployed.

The Greek Revolution of 1821, and the long War of Independence which followed, radically changed the destiny of the island. With other islands, Hydra had contributed its navy to the Revolution. And the extensive wealth accumulated in the past by the community and the island's prominent families had been generously given to the national cause. At the end of the war in the late 1820's, Hydra found itself a part of independent Greece, its privileged autonomy under Turkish rule exchanged for complete national independence.

Hydra's prominent families continued to play an important role in the political affairs of the new nation, but the island, because of its new affiliations and the changed international situation, never again saw the prosperity it had enjoyed at the turn of the century. The population declined; other commercial centers grew; and the steamship dealt the final blow to the economy of the island.

# PART II
# THE DEVELOPMENT OF THE TOWN

Episkopi. Photograph taken during the summer of 1963.

## EPISKOPI

It is not surprising that the first settlement on Hydra was organized at Episkopi, on an inland site far from the sea and concealed from the observation of passing ships. The early settlers, farmers and shepherds, obviously regarded the sea as an alien element. They had learned from experience that their chances for survival were better if their existence was unknown to outsiders.

Episkopi was not destined to become the major settlement on the island since the natural conditions did not favor such a development. But even before this became evident the village was destroyed by what seems to have been a pirate raid. Today a small settlement of about sixty-eight people occupies the same site.

## CHOICE OF SITE

Those who settled on the island later and in larger numbers possibly never gave up the idea of returning to their lands of origin. For them, both symbolically and physically, the site of the settlement had to be near the water. The sea was a link with their old homes as well as their only means of contact with the outside world.

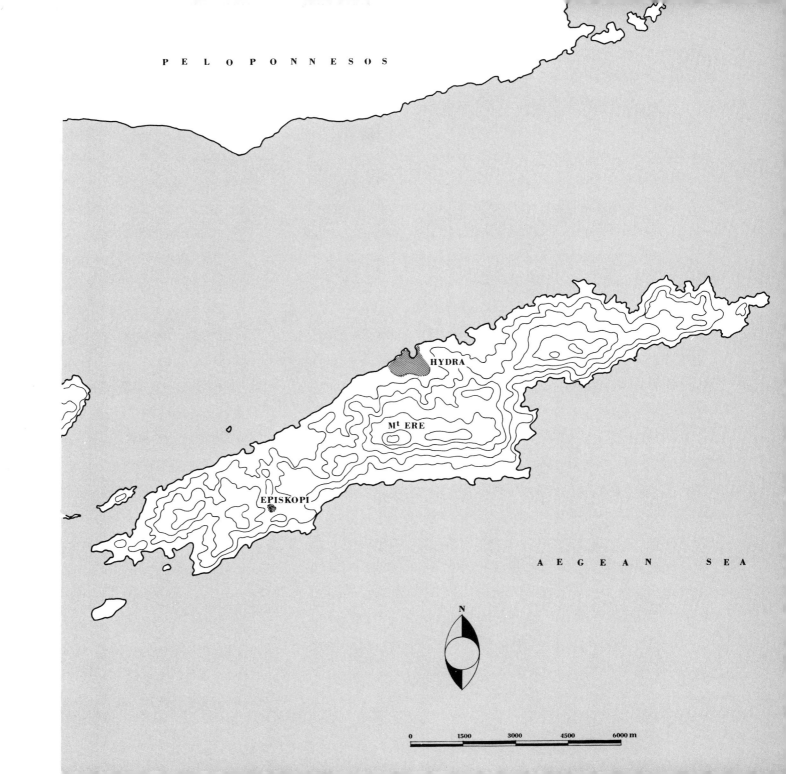

P E L O P O N N E S O S

HYDRA

Mᵗ ERE

EPISKOPI

A E G E A N     S E A

N

0      1500      3000      4500      6000 m

Map of Hydra with topographic
contour lines.

Looking at the topographic map of the island one immediately realizes that the general character of Hydra's south side—very precipitous and completely exposed—does not lend itself to a port settlement. The north side, however, provides a number of alternatives, though none of them is ideal.

The choice of the present town site was greatly influenced by location and topographic considerations, but it was also reinforced by an accidental event—the erection of a monastery in the 1640's[1] at the deepest point of the natural port. Quite possibly some houses were built in this vicinity before that date, but such a building was a strong factor in establishing the primacy of this site over others. There is no record of the reason the monastery was built at this location, although it is known that it was founded by a nun from the island of Kythnos. Considering the roaming pirates of that time, building next to the water's edge hardly seems an act of great wisdom. But the disregard of that danger in choosing the site may be an indication of how little known the island was to the outside world.

The site also had one important advantage over others: its proximity to the top of Mount Ere. There a guard, always scanning the approaches to the island, could detect and immediately report any suspicious move on the sea within a radius of sixty miles. In later years this post was used for sighting Hydriot ships in advance of their appearance in port.

The gradual slope of the terrain ascending from the bay was another favorable characteristic of the site. This gradual ascent from the water provided a large area for future expansion of the settlement. It is possible that the settlers intuited the future growth of the town in their consideration of a location.

The disadvantages of a northern exposure (subject to seasonal rough seas) may have been overlooked by the settlers, since as shepherds and farmers they were not familiar with such matters. But, considering the alternatives, the final choice was a reasonable one.

## THE SITE: ITS EARLY DEVELOPMENT

A defensible location was a matter of life and death to an Aegean settlement during the seventeenth and eighteenth centuries. A high elevation and a commanding view of the accesses—thus minimizing the chances of a surprise attack by pirates—were bare essentials, and this site provided them. Three areas around the bay (A, B, C) at first glance seem to satisfy the defense requirements. The area east of the bay (B), however, suffers from exposure to the hot western sun during the summer and is also very precipitous. The area selected (C) has a definite advantage over the one west of the port (A) because of its proximity to a source of water at its eastern end.

---

[1] For a number of years it housed an order of nuns, but a few decades after its establishment it was converted to a monastery and operated as such until the 1820's.

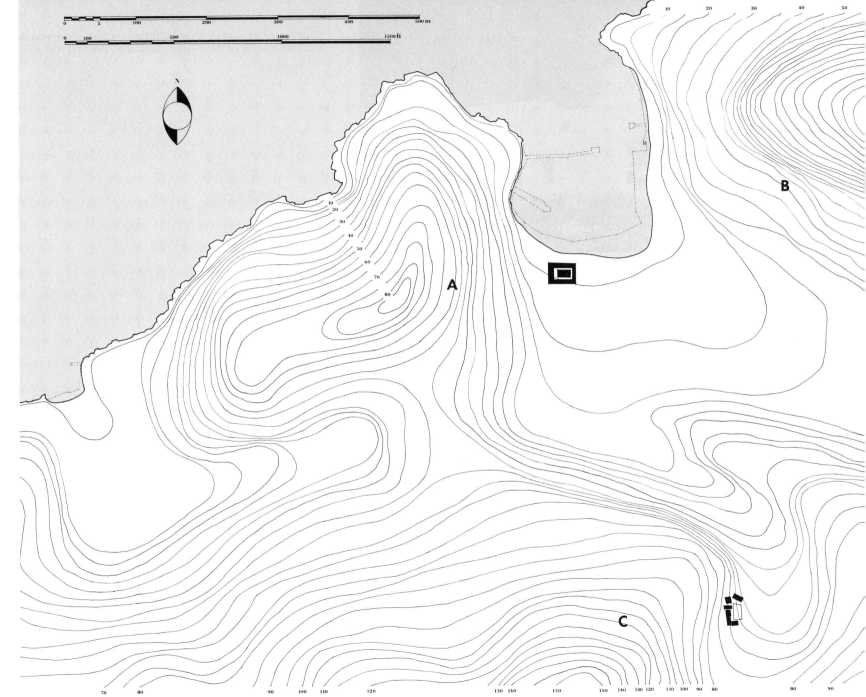

The site: contour lines at five-meter intervals indicate its topographic character. The monastery is shown near the sea. The future Twin Wells are also shown at the lower right of the plan.

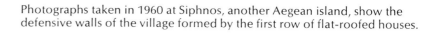

Photographs taken in 1960 at Siphnos, another Aegean island, show the defensive walls of the village formed by the first row of flat-roofed houses.

The original settlement was named Kiafa, and George D. Kriezis, a nineteenth-century historian of the island, writes that around 1680 it consisted of 370 houses. Assuming an average of five persons per family, and that a "house" represented one family, the population can be estimated at about 1,850 persons. Kiafa is almost totally deserted today, and the old houses lie in ruins. The town has moved to the lower parts of the site. But from these ruins, from the few remaining houses at the edges of the town, and from a number of eighteenth- and nineteenth-century illustrations, it can be ascertained that the old part of the town shared features common to all contemporary Aegean settlements.

One of the few surviving houses of Kiafa. Note how the house bridges over the street, a common feature in Kiafa.

Arched street in Kiafa. Note the roughly hewn ceiling beams.

Party walls served to transform the first row of houses parallel to the topographic contours into a system of defensive walls. The flat roofs served in times of need as continuous ramparts, and arched streets allowed the defenders freedom of movement. The limited number of openings in the outside walls of the houses and the controlled entrances to the total compound emphasized the defensive aspects of the settlement.

The town's narrow streets allowed for compression of the town's size, thereby shortening the defense perimeter. And the odd shapes of the streets, dictated mainly by the topography, provided a time-honored defensive advantage

33

for the town: an enemy who managed to penetrate the defense perimeter would be confused and disoriented, like Thucydides' Thebans in Platea, by the unfamiliar labyrinth. Comfort as well as defense was offered by these streets, which were mostly shaded during Hydra's hot summer months.

A continuous east-west path which still survives today supports the notion that the first row of houses on the south side of the settlement served as an exterior defensive wall. Following the site contours, the path also served as a "collector" for all north-south paths leading downhill, by channeling the traffic toward a source of water (the Twin Wells, discussed in Part III) at the eastern end, and toward the few cultivated fields, most of which were located west of the settlement.

The path connecting Kiafa and the port followed the principle of minimum effort. It descended the hill at a place where the slope is most gradual, and as it reached the land saddle southwest of the port it turned east, again following the most gradual slope, to the west side of the monastery. It was natural that the path to the most important building of the town should conform with the traditional requirement that the entrance to the monastery be on its western side.

Another important path originated from the water source. It led down to the east side of the monastery and was obviously used primarily for carrying water to supply the ships.

These paths ran parallel to the east and west sides of the monastery and opened up into the area north of the building to form an important space. This is where the ships loaded and unloaded; this is where all commercial transactions took place during working hours. In addition, this space was next to the most important public building of the town · and therefore was destined to form the nucleus of its future civic center.

This diagram, together with those on pages 37 and 39, is intended to show graphically the probable form and size of the town of Hydra, relating it to the extent of the sea travels of the Hydriots and to the predominant type of vessel used by them, during three successive stages of Hydra's development. Note that in this first stage the Hydriots traveled only within the Aegean Sea, that they used a very small type of vessel, and that the town was still a tightly put together defensive settlement. The ships reproduced on pages 35 and 37 are details taken from the painting which appears on page 22. Courtesy Historic Archives of Hydra.

# HYDRA 1650-1750

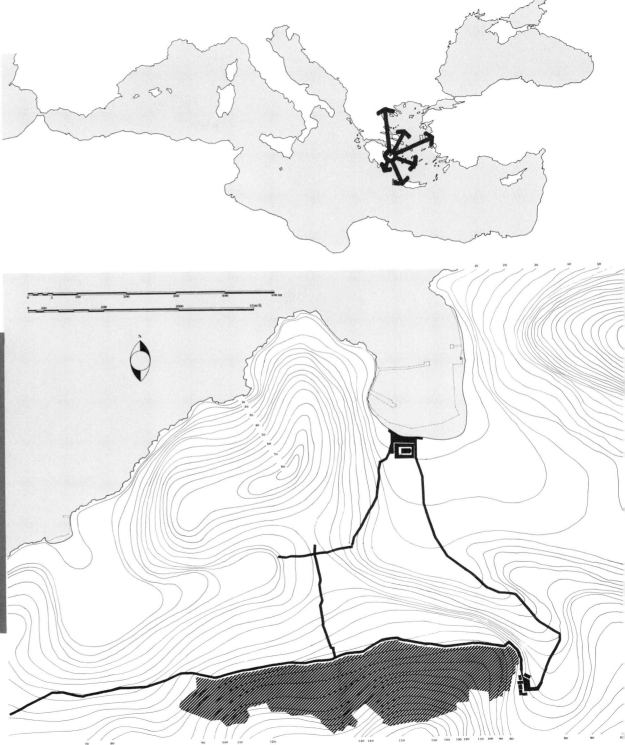

## YEARS OF GROWTH

Wars in the Peloponnesos brought successive waves of refugees to the island during the first half of the eighteenth century, intensifying the problem of its limited natural resources. Around 1750 the population of the town consisted of 604 families, or about 3,000 persons. By this time the society of farmers and shepherds had given up its old ways and had changed into a society of sea traders.

The problems of the settlement now took a different orientation. In the first place, to accommodate the population increase the town had to expand. In the second place, the population increase meant an expansion of Hydra's sea power, as there were more men to man more ships. The combination of these circumstances resulted in the dilution of the old, strictly defensive character of the settlement, since a town of 3,000 persons with a prospering and powerful navy at its disposition will not be an easy prey to a pirate raid. This newly acquired sense of relative security allowed the development of the town beyond its protective "walls." As sea commerce grew, more and more of the town's life took place near the port. Thus the old settlement expanded toward the port.

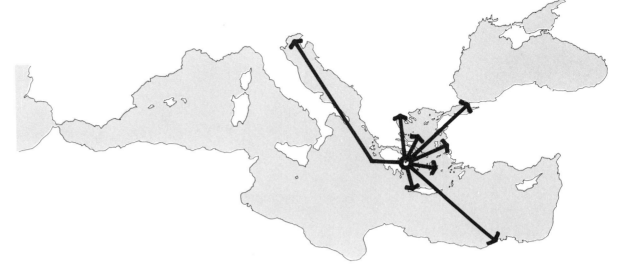

In this second stage of development, larger Hydriot ships reached the Black Sea, Alexandria, and Trieste, and the town expanded beyond its original defense perimeter.

# HYDRA 1750-1774

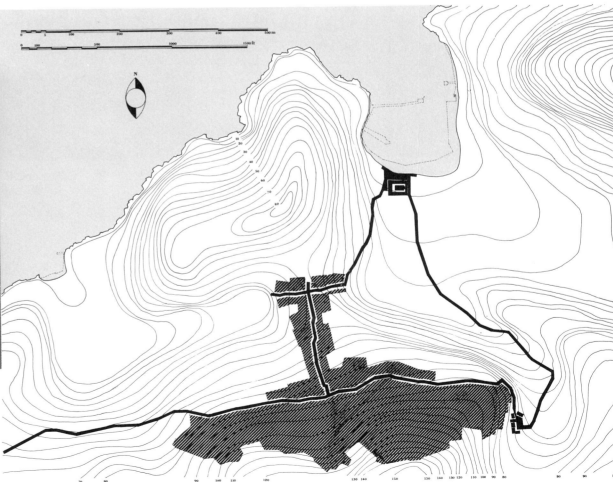

View of Hydra at the end of the eighteenth century, reproduced from A. L. Castellan. *Lettres sur la Morée* (Paris, 1808). The view looks north from the Twin Wells area (see Part III, Twin Wells study).

During the last decades of the eighteenth century prominent families began to emerge as a result of many profitable sea ventures. These wealthy families built *archontica*, large private residences which required more space than the densely constructed Kiafa could afford. The greatest number of *archontica* were built in an area immediately west of the port where an elevated site accented the prominence of these families in the life of the town.

In addition, the area was protected from the western sun and lay in the general direction of the town's expansion.

The population of the town in 1765 was 667 families, and in 1770, 706 families, or about 3,500 persons. The census of 1794, which reflected the large influx of refugees from the Russo-Turkish Wars of 1768–74, showed 2,235 houses and a population of more than 11,000.

The forty-one-year period between 1774 and 1815 was the

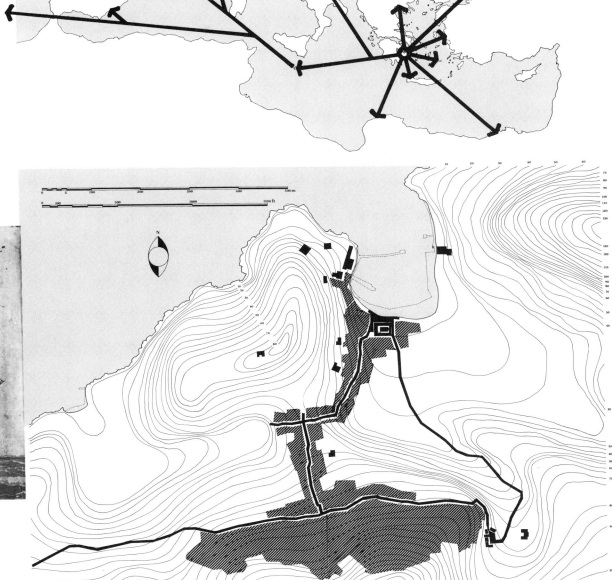

As Hydriot brigs sailed from the Black Sea to western Mediterranean ports (some beyond Gibraltar), the town reached its last and most important stage of development. Note some of the *archontica* shown immediately west of the port. A sizable brig·(*Achilles*, watercolor signed by Antoine Roux of Marseille, 1819) flying the Russian flag is shown here. Brigs, together with three-masted barks, were the predominant type of vessel used by the Hydriots at this time.

# HYDRA 1774-1815

Aerial photograph of the island and the town. The monastery of Prophet Elias is shown at the top of the hill to the right. The top of Mount Ere is shown at the extreme right-hand corner of the picture.

time of Hydra's great economic boom. The prosperity of these years produced, essentially, the town's present form. However, two further minor changes did occur before the final consolidation of Hydra as it is today. The first of these changes was the partial development of the area west of the town over the saddle, which probably resulted from a population overspill during the 1820's. These were the years of the Greek War of Independence, when a new influx of refugees swelled the population of the town to a total of 28,500. The second event was the almost complete abandonment of Kiafa, because the conditions which necessitated a settlement on a high elevation no longer existed, and because the population had declined substantially in later years.

The town plan with superimposed topographic contour lines at five meters. Data for this plan was taken during the summer of 1963. Note the ruined walls of the deserted houses of Kiafa in the lower middle portion of the drawing.

N

500 m
1500 ft

Three views of the town in sequence from low elevation point, to middle, to high.

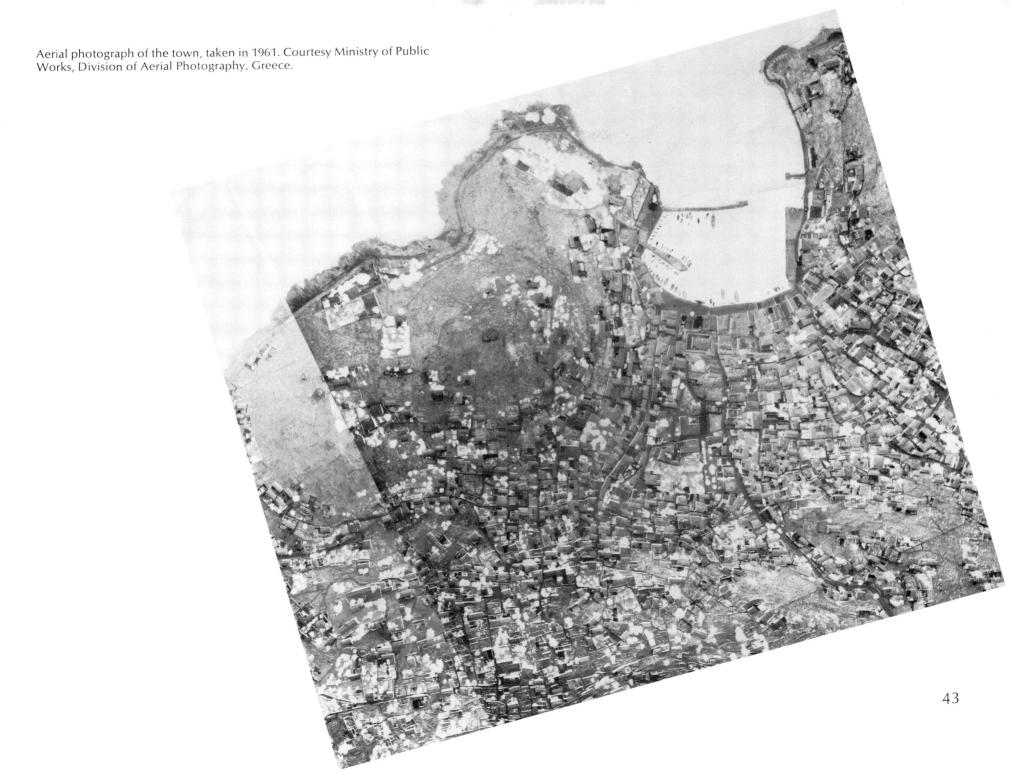

Aerial photograph of the town, taken in 1961. Courtesy Ministry of Public Works, Division of Aerial Photography, Greece.

43

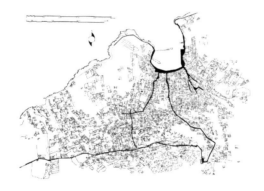

The plan of Hydra is shown in the same scale as the plan of Washington, D.C. (right), including the Mall, the Capitol, the White House, and the Pentagon building; the plan of St. Peter's in Rome (upper left); and the plan of St. Mark's Square in Venice (lower left).

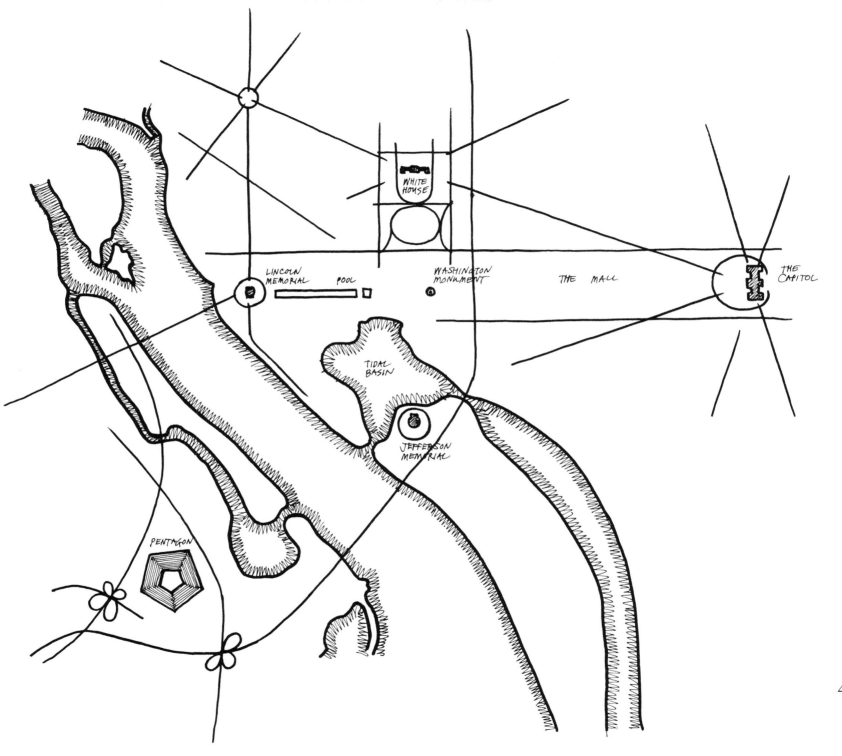

WHITE
HOUSE

LINCOLN
MEMORIAL          POOL                    WASHINGTON
                                         MONUMENT          THE   MALL                    THE
                                                                                         CAPITOL

                              TIDAL
                              BASIN

                                    JEFFERSON
                                    MEMORIAL

PENTAGON

# THE FORM OF THE TOWN

If one is to compare the diagrams of Hydra's historic growth with one another, one thing becomes immediately apparent: the original decisions described at the beginning of this chapter—the building of the monastery near the port, the choice of Kiafa as the site for settlement, and the path network created by the interrelationships of these two centers of activity—produced a basic skeleton, a structuring frame, so to speak, which the growing town faithfully followed by "filling in" the predetermined areas. What this skeleton and "fill in" process produced is the present form of the town, a form which is strongly reminiscent of the classical theater.

At first this association of forms may seem to stem from a rather formalistic attitude, but it is worth a more careful examination. The theater can be singled out of all classical structures as the one completely adapted to site conditions, as opposed, for example, to the Greek temple concept of clearly distinguishing nature from man-made architecture.

The very form of the theater evolved from site considerations. Religious rites originally required a flat dancing place, with a slope rising above it to accommodate the onlookers. But the final form of the classical theater as we know it, with its geometric articulation, stepped seats, proscenium, scene, and so forth, while strictly adhering to the original site considerations, emerged as a result of

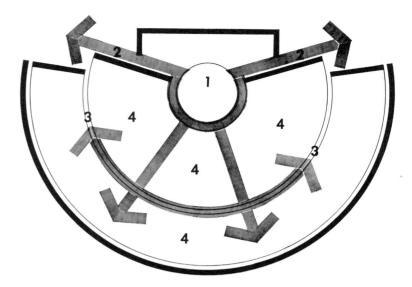

Schematic plan of the Epidauros Theater: 1. *Orchestra*; 2. *Parodos*; 3. *Diazoma*; 4. *Theatron*.

a transformation, that is, the secularization of its content.

In Hydra, too, site considerations were, from the very beginning, paramount. The final form of the town emerged as its society went through a period of transformation, but this final form was as much a result of site considerations as the original one.

The similarities between the classical theater and the town form are rather intriguing. Both the orchestra in the former and the port in the latter have the symbolic and physical attributes of entries to their respective complexes. At the same time, the *orchestra* is the focus of the theater and the port is the center of life in the town. The major access to

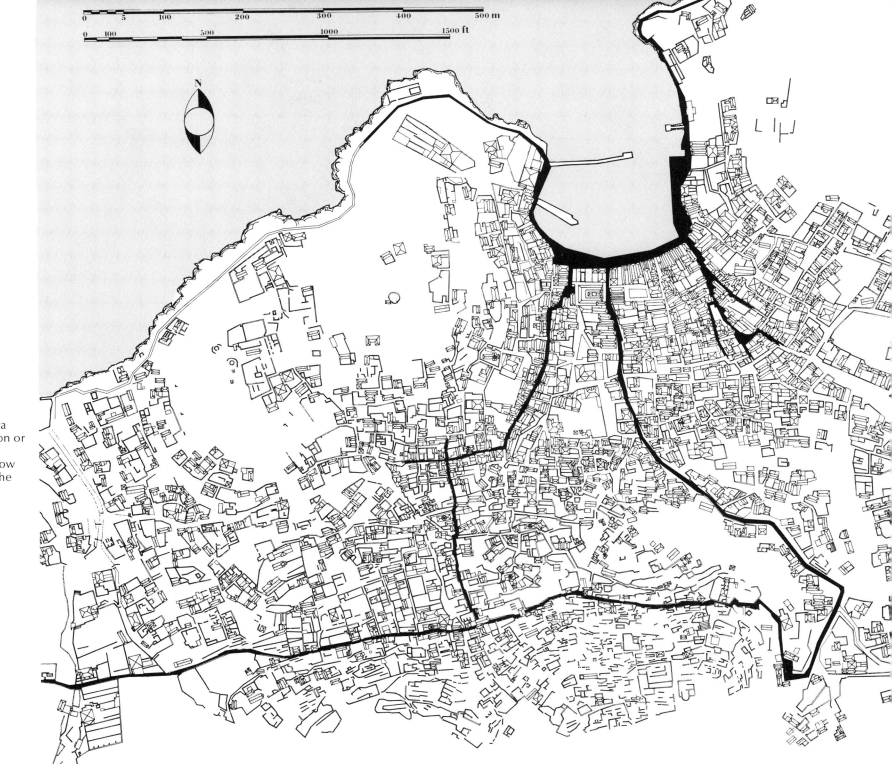

The town plan of Hydra shown with the skeleton or structural frame superimposed. Note how the city fabric fills in the areas in between.

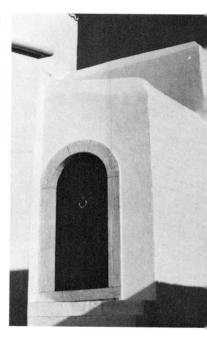

Views of Hydra's streets. Note the special relationship of house entrances to the axis of the street.

and from the area of the port follows both the *parodos* and the up-and-down aisle pattern of the theater. The *diazoma* finds its equivalent in the "collector path" at the foot of Kiafa; and the stepped seats of the *theatron* proper become the clusters of house units.

I do not wish to argue that the town was developed according to a preconceived design. Hydra definitely belongs to the category of "grown" towns. If there is a point to be made here it should be this: the strong character of the site was predominant in producing the form of the town. This form, so similar to that of the classical theater, had the significant advantage of being a perceptible form, a form understandable and recognizable to all its citizens. Every step taken in building the town was consistent with its basic theme and a contribution to its total image.

The city fabric in Hydra is defined by the individual house

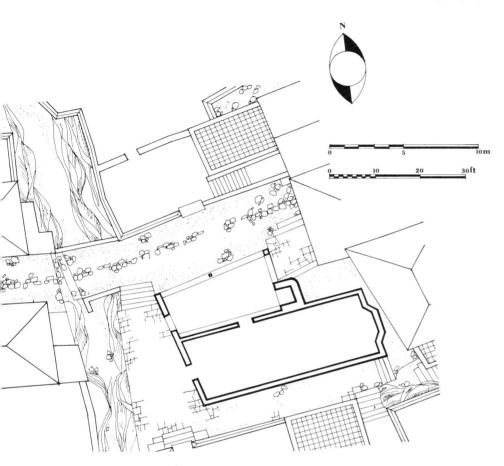

Plan of the church of Evangelismos and its immediate neighborhood in the upper part of the town. Note the relationship of the porch to the street and the church.

Neighborhood path leading to the door on the north wall of the church of St. Constantine.

units. The way these house units are joined into the over-all skeleton is obviously critical. These joints, that is the entries to the individual houses, become even more critical as a result of the particular treatment they receive in Hydra: in a great many cases the entry is turned to face the visitor as he arrives from the port, rather than to comply with the normal pattern of facing the axis of the street. Such a departure from the normal pattern can only be explained

as stemming from the intimate relationship in the minds of Hydriots between the house unit and the perceptible form of the town.

Churches are numerous in Hydra. Quite a few are "family" churches, though most of them served as parish churches at one time or another. As a result, neighborhood and town form considerations frequently caused a departure from the strict laws of the architecture of the

49

A

Views from various points on the periphery of the town.

B

Eastern Church. Traditionally, the altar is on the east side and the main entry to the church is on the west side.[2] In some cases an entry on the south side, with or without a porch, supplements or replaces the usual west-side entry, while the north side is conventionally a solid wall or one lightly perforated by windows.

This traditional treatment of the north wall is not respected in the church of St. Constantine, where an entry door opens on the north. The reason for such a violation is, I believe, that this door is also placed at the end of a long access path to the church in an effort to relate it directly to its immediate neighborhood. In the church of Evangelismos a porch is attached on the north side. Here, too, strict

[2] In Hydra, as in all Aegean islands, the predominant type of church is that of the basilica with a great number of minor variations.

D E F

architectural tradition is violated in an obvious effort to relate this porch to the major street beside the church. In this manner the porch also opens up symbolically toward the port.

In Part III of this study a significant component of the town, the "Twin Wells," will be discussed in detail. It is appropriate to say here, however, that the manner in which this particular space is formed again echoes the perceptible amphitheatrical form of the town.

The town in its horizontal projection seems to lose the geometric strength of the amphitheatrical plan at its periphery. But in reality it is at such places that the over-all form of the town becomes fully apparent. Here successive and surprising vistas through narrow openings present the form in unmistakable terms as shown in the sequence of photographs above.

51

The rock next to the entry of a house (above left) is considered part of the house and is whitewashed with the rest of it. In another instance (center left) it becomes part of the wall of the house and part of the balcony balustrade. The top of a private space enclosure (bottom left) follows the variations of the public street and produces an intriguing plastic form.

## THE FUNCTION OF THE TOWN

In the preceding pages the over-all perceptible form of Hydra has been discussed. But the student of its morphological development will recognize that the town also indicates the extreme adaptability of its parts to the demands of the particular site. Indeed, the process of adjusting the building to the site and the site to the building was a specific and predominant form-giving device for the town. This adaptability of parts to particular site situations allows us to classify these parts according to their specific topographic feature.

Kiafa emerged as a *town on a slope*. The collector street and the orientation of its houses complied with the premises of such a classification. As the town grew, its new parts utilized the feature of a *saddle town*. It did not develop as a saddle town, however, because of the nearby, stronger center of attraction: the port. The concentration of the *archontica* in the area west of the port had the overtones of a belated *hilltop town* development, while in the part which developed last, characteristics of a *valley town* were predominant.[3]

What dominated the life of the town in all its stages, of course, was the sea. Hydra was always a port town. But this classification should be explained.

[3] See Ernst Egli, *Climate and Town Districts* (Erlenbach-Zurich: Verlag für Architektur, 1951), pp. 110–26. I am indebted to him for the classifications listed above.

Diagram of the town
showing possible
classification of its parts
according to the definitions
used by Ernst Egli in
*Climate and Town Districts*:
1. Town on a slope;
2. Saddle town;
3. Hilltop town;
4. Valley town.

The quay shown functioning as a commercial center in the morning (left);
a commercial and social center at noon—note restaurants, cafés (center);
and as a religious center during a religious holiday (right).

Although a port, Hydra never served an inland region beyond itself. Consequently, it did not develop as an industrial, manufacturing, or transportation center. Neither did it develop the usual features of a port town—warehouses, inland communications, and so forth—a fact which allowed its society to continue practically unchanged despite the events of the last decades of the eighteenth and the first of the nineteenth centuries. Very few non-Hydriot ships ever used the port. In essence, Hydra served as a dormitory, a breeding and retirement place for the crews, and a shipbuilding, maintenance, and repair center for its own fleet. Its shipyards filled orders only for Hydriots, and its manufacturing facilities never extended beyond production of food supplies, ropes, sails, and so forth, for its own ships.

The town owes its sudden rise to fame and importance to certain extraordinary circumstances. When these circumstances changed, the island lost its prominent position in Mediterranean life, retaining only its dignified form.[4] This form survives today for tourists, but its parts retain their traditional human uses.

The austere continuous semicircular façade wall which encompasses the port and its activities also serves as a physical separation of two distinctly different functions, public on one side and private on the other. The quay is the center of activity for the town in a multiple sense. During the early part of the day it serves as a commercial center, while late in the day it becomes a social center. On holidays and days of public celebration it becomes a formal civic center.

A limited number of small openings which penetrate this continuous façade lead to the residential sectors. The scale and character of the environment change dramatically beyond

[4] As such an example, Hydra does not stand alone: the island of Nantucket, off the coast of Massachusetts, is at least one similar case.

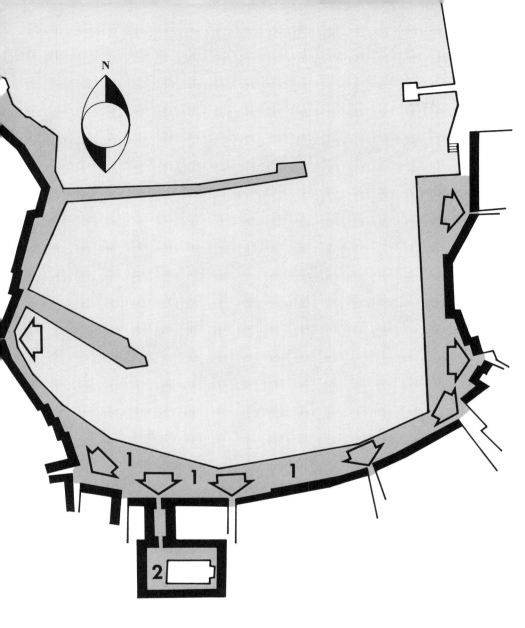

The heavy line indicates the continuous semicircular façade separating public areas from areas of private use. Note the continuity between the commercial-social center (1) and the governmental-religious center (2)—both shown shaded—and the way these spaces are articulated (see Part III, monastery study).

these openings. Usually narrow, stepped streets carry the pedestrian traffic[5] and link the main center of activity of the town with the individual residential units.

At the widest part of the quay an opening which leads to the monastery establishes a physical connection between the commercial space on its north side and the governmental and religious center of the town on the south. Thus an articulate continuity between these spaces is established.

The first of the two land use plans shows the disposition of the *archontica*, churches (both parish and family), and educational institutions. The second plan illustrates the disposition of government buildings, shops, stores, and public accommodations in general. Most of them are concentrated around the port, an area which has been traditionally allocated for similar functions. This concentration testifies to the existence of an intuitive distinction between what is a public and what a private function, and to a decisive separation of each. It also reinforces the notion that the town operates as a singular entity. Those stores shown scattered at various locations are "corner stores," serving the small needs of the immediate neighborhood and always related to the neighborhood through an important architectural feature, usually a paved opening with a shade-providing tree in the middle.

[5] There are no vehicles in the town, although during the summer of 1963 a truck was used for a construction project. This truck, which could barely pass through one of the penetrations of the continuous façade, was intended to be removed from the island once the project was finished.

Land use plan showing the
*archontica* (heavy outline),
schools (lines and dot),
and churches (black).

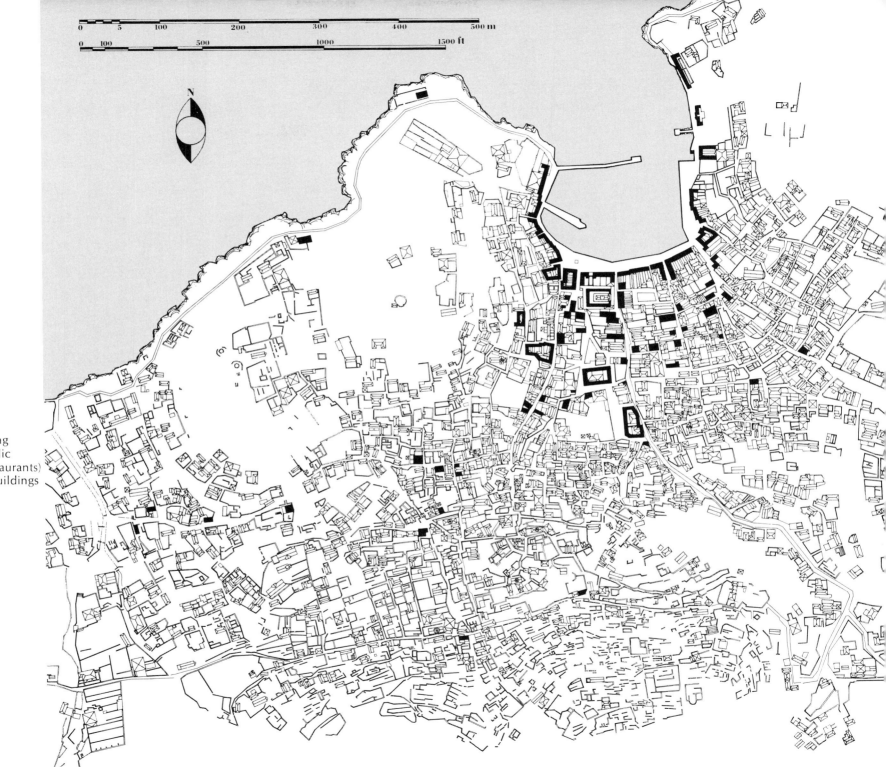

Land use plan showing
stores and other public
facilities (hotels, restaurants)
and governmental buildings
(national and local
government).

# PART III
# THE COMPONENTS OF THE TOWN

While the idea of the perceptible form of the town has already been extensively discussed, the notion of the consistency of its parts was only suggested. Hydra's impressive form is derived equally from both elements. It is a perceptible form carried out consistently through a wide range of scales: the scale of the town, the scale of the neighborhood, the scale of a street, the scale of the individual house, and so forth. We have here, then, a well understood, conceptual frame within which the individual builder found room to adjust and perform intuitively according to the specific conditions of his problem.

Consequently, when speaking of Hydra's form one should speak of it as an entity of complementary parts. One should speak of its structuring concept as well as of the way the individual houses are organized, of the way clusters of houses are interrelated, of the way public streets and paths are formed, public spaces generated and contained, of how streets are paved, windows framed, stones laid to make a wall, doors painted, or color used. It is a town organized in an Albertian sense, in which none of the parts could be omitted without a detrimental effect to the whole. With this notion in mind, an attempt has been made to study in detail a number of the important components of the town.

As indicated on the plan, two clusters of houses were chosen for study: one rests on a relatively flat site, the other on a strongly sloping one. Next a street and its auxiliaries were studied; then a space of architectural as well as social importance, the Twin Wells. A representative *archontico* was chosen for study next; and the study concludes with the monastery, an important building in the town historically as well as in terms of urban design.

Areas of detailed study
are circled to indicate their
position in the general
town plan:
A. Cluster of Houses I;
B. Cluster of Houses II;
C. Street study;
D. Twin Wells;
E. Voulgaris' House;
F. Monastery.

Cluster of Houses I: sections through public streets surrounding the cluster.

## CLUSTER OF HOUSES I

This cluster of houses belongs to that part of Hydra which was formed during the last stage of its development, in the first half of the nineteenth century. The cluster occupies an almost flat site. It was chosen for study because it is enclosed by four streets in a roughly ninety degree relationship to one another. Because of this it resembles a typical non-Hydriot residential city block more than any other cluster in this part of the town.

Its dimensions are approximately 145 by 165 feet, enclosing an area of about 24,000 square feet. This cluster, occupied by 16 residential units, has a density of 29 families per acre. The two-level arrangement of the cluster is typical of the great majority of houses in the town, although some houses are built on one level. The very few cases of three-level houses are dictated by topographic considerations (sloping site) and are, therefore, absent from the particular cluster under discussion.

As mentioned before, Hydra is a "grown" town. Its growth was never controlled by a "master plan" or a building code. The building controls were part of an unwritten tradition of

Cluster of Houses I: plan. Arrows indicate entrances to individual properties. Note the L-shaped dead-end access at the upper left-hand corner of site.

60

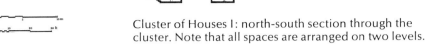

Cluster of Houses I: north-south section through the cluster. Note that all spaces are arranged on two levels.

Cluster of Houses I: diagram identifying sixteen different properties comprising the cluster.

community interests, family privacy, or construction details. In building a new house, the first concern of the builder, who in many cases was the owner himself, was that the building not interfere with the use of an already established public path. From that point on he had as much freedom as the particular features of the site would allow. Orientation played a secondary role to the issues of adjusting the house to the site and the site to the house. Irregularly shaped streets resulted from the fact that no attempt was made to keep straight building lines. The party-wall system was widely used, particularly in areas where high density was desirable.

Each house in the cluster under study represents one family, that is, parents and unmarried children. When a son or daughter was married, a new house was required for them. This new house was then built within the uncovered space of the parental lot, although it was treated as a separate unit and given a direct entry from the public street. This process gave rise to odd lot shapes and dead-end accesses such as the L-shaped lot off the west side of the cluster under discussion. Horizontal ownership, in which one family owns the lower floor and another the upper floor, also has a number of

61

Sequence of twelve photographs taken around Cluster of Houses I. Diagram on the right identifies the position from which each numbered photograph was taken.

1

2

3

4

5

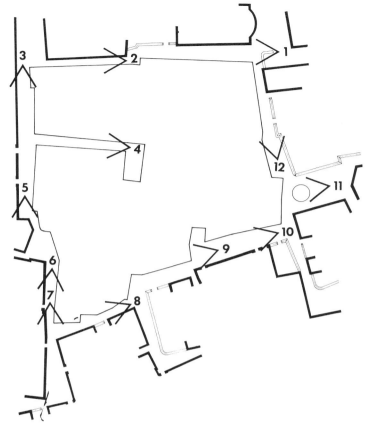

7    8    9    10    11    12

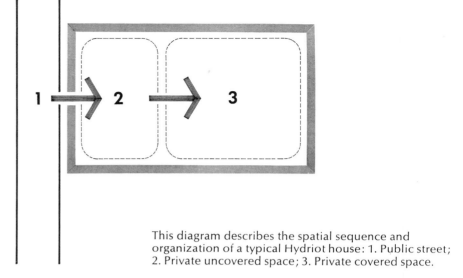

This diagram describes the spatial sequence and organization of a typical Hydriot house: 1. Public street; 2. Private uncovered space; 3. Private covered space.

applications in Hydra, offering an alternative to the new house for a new couple when empty land was not available.

A morphologically important, unifying factor in the cluster is the shape of the individual house—a simple rectangular or L-shaped container. Available materials and methods of construction (stone walls, timber roofs and floors) dictated this shape. But an even more important unifying factor is the clearly established spatial sequence leading to the individual house. This sequence can be described as follows: public street —penetration—private uncovered space—penetration— private enclosed space (house proper). This sequence applies to all but two of the sixteen residential units of this cluster. Generally speaking, it is the most important formative principle of the typical Hydriot house.

The house shown in detail is representative of the houses of Hydra both in terms of its shape and in terms of the previously described spatial sequence. It is organized on two levels and

it is possible that it was originally built as a simple rectangle (north-south branch) and later expanded to an L-shaped unit. There is direct access from the court to both floors.

Individual spaces within the house, rather than following the rigid principle of upper floor private areas, lower floor reception areas, conform to "topographic" considerations. The kitchen is located downstairs because of the oven, cistern, and well, while the living and reception room is placed upstairs where its three different exposures (south, west, and north) overlook the public street and the house court. Bedrooms are on both floors.

It is of interest to note that the openings in the south wall look over the court of another property. Quite possibly these two adjacent properties were once one, but were separated when a family marriage created a need for another house.

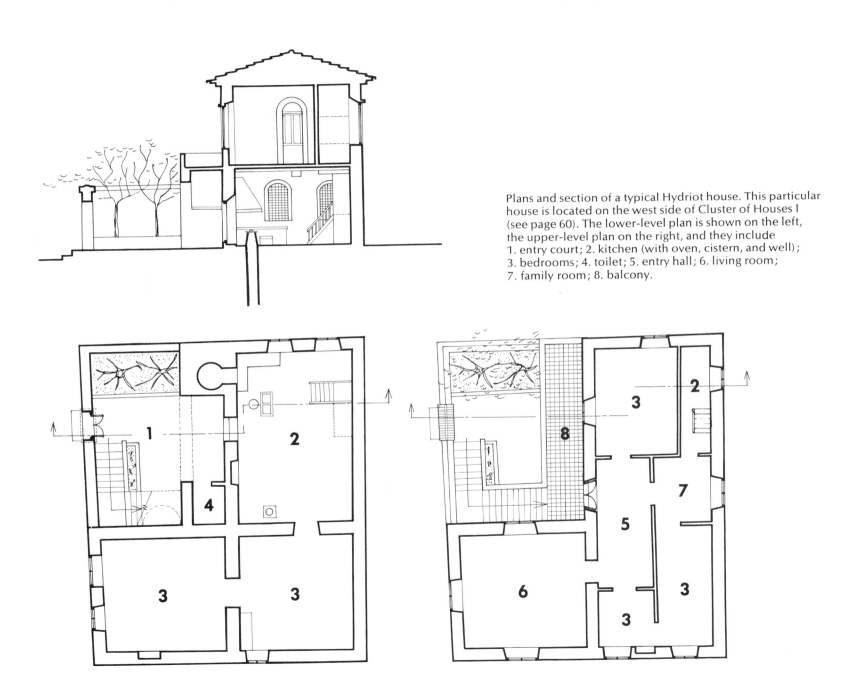

Plans and section of a typical Hydriot house. This particular house is located on the west side of Cluster of Houses I (see page 60). The lower-level plan is shown on the left, the upper-level plan on the right, and they include
1. entry court; 2. kitchen (with oven, cistern, and well);
3. bedrooms; 4. toilet; 5. entry hall; 6. living room;
7. family room; 8. balcony.

Plans of a house from Cluster of Houses II. Note at the ground level (bottom) the public path which is bridged over by the upper level of the house (top).

The photograph on the left shows a number of individually owned houses coming together in a cluster located on a relatively flat site. The photograph on the right shows how another cluster has disintegrated on a sloping site. Note how easy it becomes to identify individual properties on this type of site as opposed to the one on the left.

## CLUSTER OF HOUSES II

Because of its considerable slope, the site of this cluster is radically different from that of the site previously discussed. As a result, the "contained" cluster which could be circumvented but not penetrated has disintegrated. Individual units can be much more easily recognized, since in most cases the unit stands by itself. The elements unifying this cluster are the small church and the rudimentary public square appended to its north side.

It is important to notice, however, that despite the disintegration of the contained cluster, the spatial sequence leading to the individual house has been retained. Indeed, for the house shown in detail the builder has made every effort (bridging over a public path) to retain this organizational

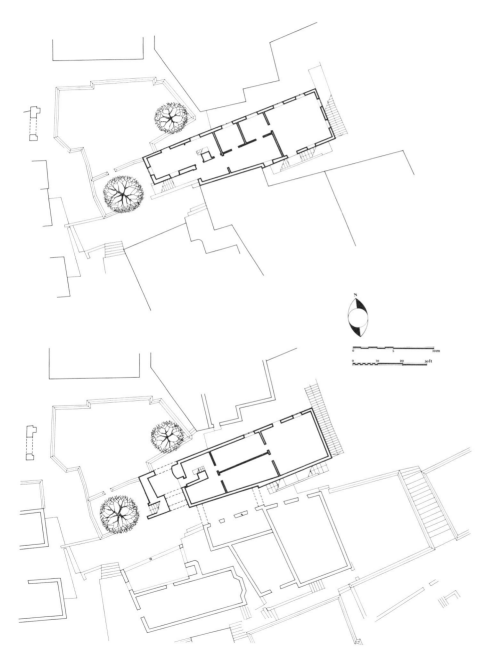

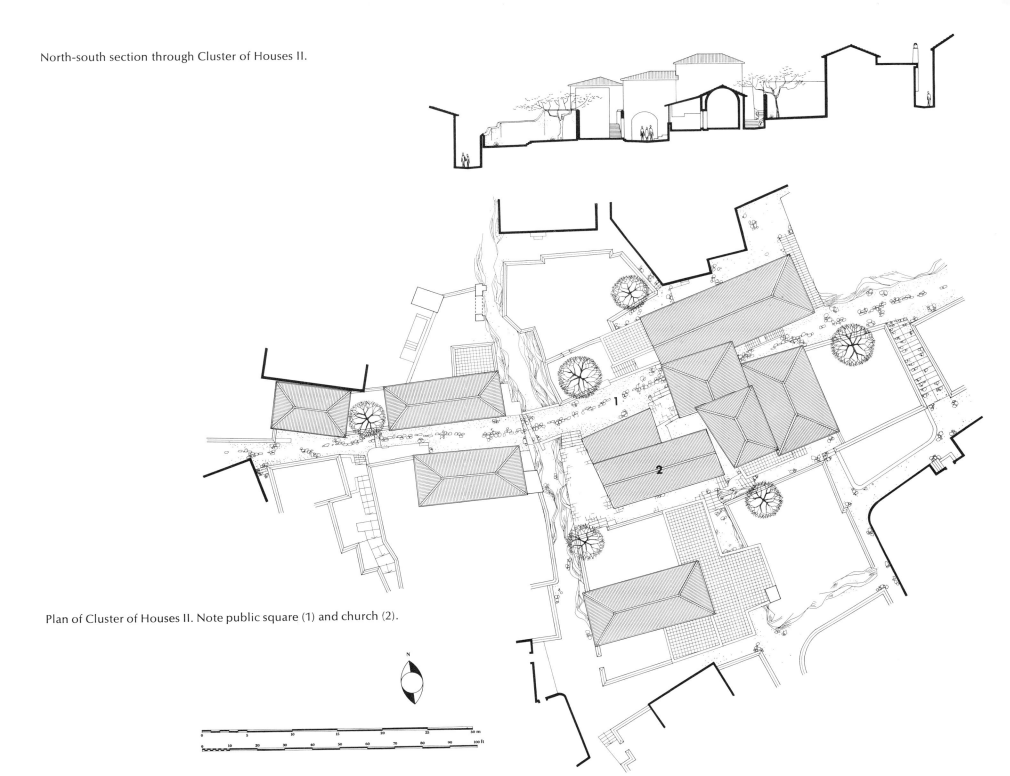

North-south section through Cluster of Houses II.

Plan of Cluster of Houses II. Note public square (1) and church (2).

N

0          5          10          15          20          25          30 m
0    10    20    30    40    50    60    70    80    90    100 ft

sequence. At the same time, all physical characteristics—
the rectangular shape and the predominantly two-level
organization—of the individual house have also been retained.

This area is occupied by seven residential units and
measures about 20,000 square feet, which brings the density
of the cluster to 15 families per acre, almost half that of the
previously described area. The steep slope of the site can
explain much of the difference, but its greater distance from
the port is another factor in lowering the over-all density.

Sequence of twelve photographs taken through the Cluster of Houses II.
Diagram on the right identifies the position from which each
numbered photograph was taken.

1   2   3   4   5   6

7             8             9             10             11             12

Streets of Hydra. Note in the extreme right photograph the forty-five-degree cut in the corner intended to facilitate traffic in the street.

A  B  C  D

## STREET STUDY

In Hydra a street or public path becomes an element of morphological importance equal to other parts of the town composition. The variety of street forms is as rich as the specific topographic conditions allow. Generally speaking, streets can be divided into two main categories: those running parallel to topographic contours and those running perpendicular to topographic contours. In the first category the ramp type is the most prevalent. The combination of ramp-step-ramp is also widely used, while a sequence of steps

F

G

H

is resorted to at intersections where abrupt elevation differences occur. In the second category, the steps-landing-steps organization is the most prevalent, but the other two methods just described are also used.

Most streets in Hydra developed first as paths leading from one point to another. Then houses were built along their sides. Finally the street was determined by adding front yards to some houses, by edging others, and by taking forty-five degree cuts at the corners of some at their ground level to allow ample ninety degree turns for the traffic.

71

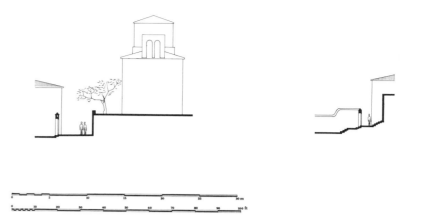

Sections perpendicular to the axis of the street.

The width of the street was determined by the volume of traffic: main arteries provided enough width for two basket-carrying beasts of burden to meet and pass, while secondary accesses provided room for one. Streets wide enough for only one person at a time are not rare. There is just one street in Hydra which is wide enough for automobile traffic, and it was constructed only recently.

In the detailed study presented here, the main pedestrian traffic axis runs parallel to the topographic contours and in an east-west direction. Secondary streets run perpendicular to these contours. A joint is formed where they all converge. This joint is acknowledged by a larger physical space with social importance: the sizeable tree in its midst, the general store on its south side, and the church on its east side contribute to the creation of its identity.

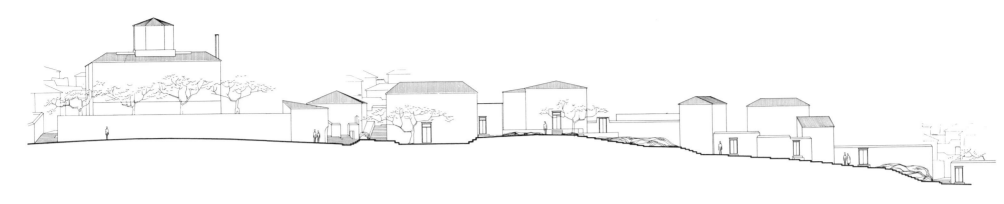

East-west section parallel to the axis of the street.

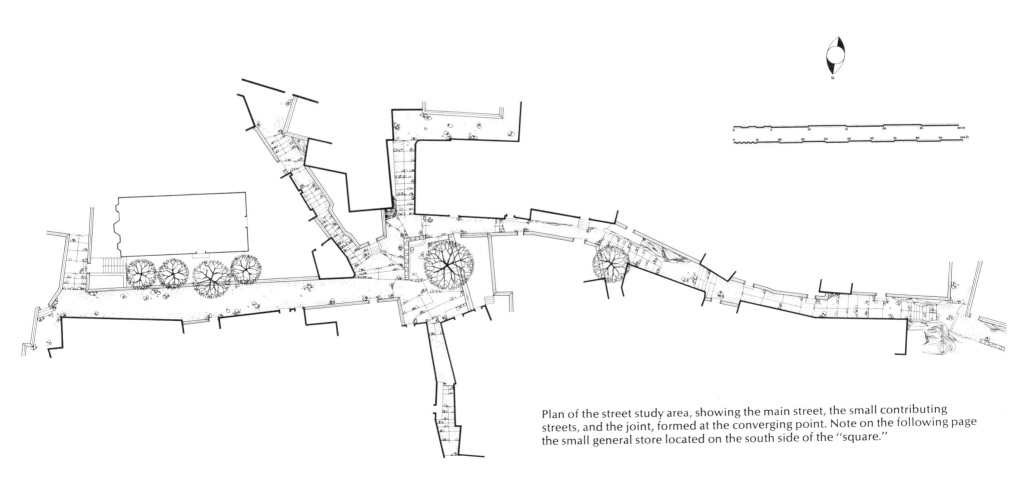

Plan of the street study area, showing the main street, the small contributing streets, and the joint, formed at the converging point. Note on the following page the small general store located on the south side of the "square."

Sequence of eight photographs taken at different positions along the axis of the street under study. These positions are identified on the diagram shown on the right.

1

2

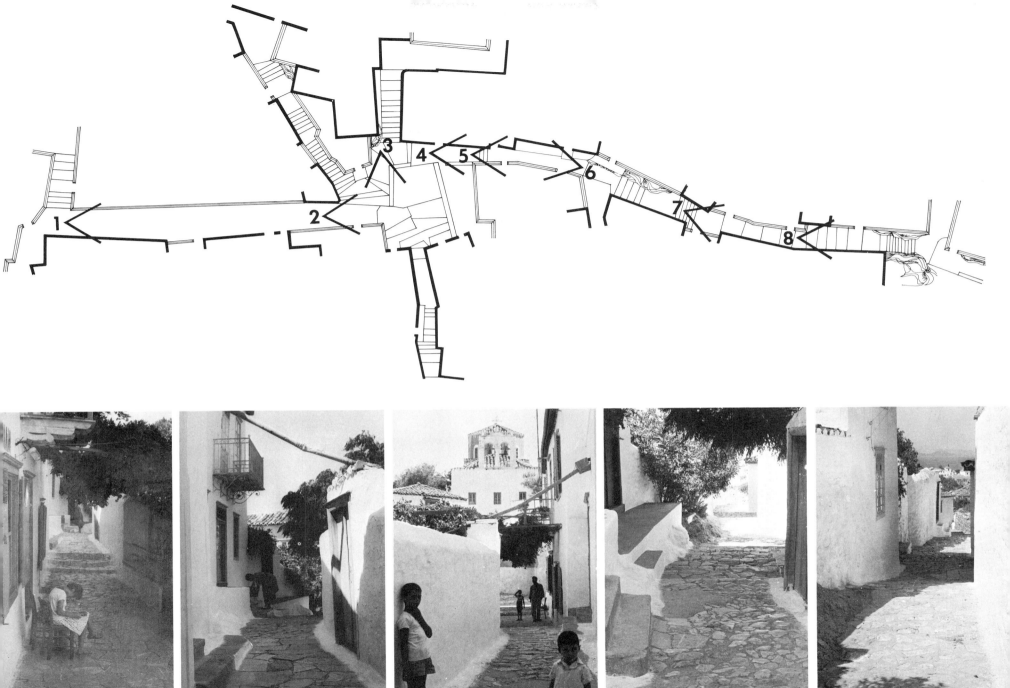

4                                 5                                 6                                 7                                 8

Twin Wells. Note the amphitheatric organization of the space. The opening and steps in the right-hand corner lead up to Kiafa.

## TWIN WELLS

This component[1] has been of great significance to the town as a source of water. While there is no historical reference to it, I see no reason why one cannot assume that water was tapped there during the early stages of the settlement's development. Because of this I have used the existence of the wells to explain the early development of Kiafa in the preceding pages.

Hydra, like a number of other Aegean settlements, has always suffered from a limited supply of water. Elaborate rain-

Twin Wells: north-south section.

water collection and storage systems were traditional devices for meeting the problem. Today, the demand for water has greatly increased because of the large number of tourists visiting the island. To meet this demand, water is brought in by floating containers from Peloponnesos, but old water sources are still in use as well. The Twin Wells produce water and act

[1] The Greek term for the place is *Kala Pigadia,* literally meaning "good wells." I argued with myself for a long time about whether it should be translated "Good Wells" or "Twin Wells." "Good well" has a universal meaning, referring to the quality of its water. In Hydra's case, I believe it was meant to establish a quality distinction from cistern water or from the brackish water of other wells nearer to the sea. "Twin wells" to my mind sounds better in English, but even more important, the term has "form" implications, and in this sense it seems to me consistent with the main concern of the study.

as a gathering place for people trading stories and news. It was to serve this dual purpose that architectural space enclosing the wells was created.

The main area of activity is defined by an elevated platform where all the elements related to this activity are organized: the openings of the wells, the trees which provide shade, and the continuous seating facilities along the base of the retaining wall. The limits of the platform are clearly defined: a series of monumental steps on its open side, retaining walls in the foreground, and continuous house façades in the background on the other three sides. A break in the façade occurs at the northwest corner of the platform in order to establish a path connection in the direction of Kiafa.

Windows and doors are punched through the house façades in an irregular pattern. The size of these openings responds to technical considerations (introduction of natural light, ventilation, thermal insulation, available materials of construction, and so forth). Both the size and the location of the openings conform to the traditional requirement for a monolithic and continuous façade which in this case enhances the concept of the enclosed architectural space. The primary colors used on these openings are consistent with the restrained character of the environment and could serve to identify different owners' property.

All in all, the three-dimensional organization of this place is strongly reminiscent of the "perceptible" form of the town.

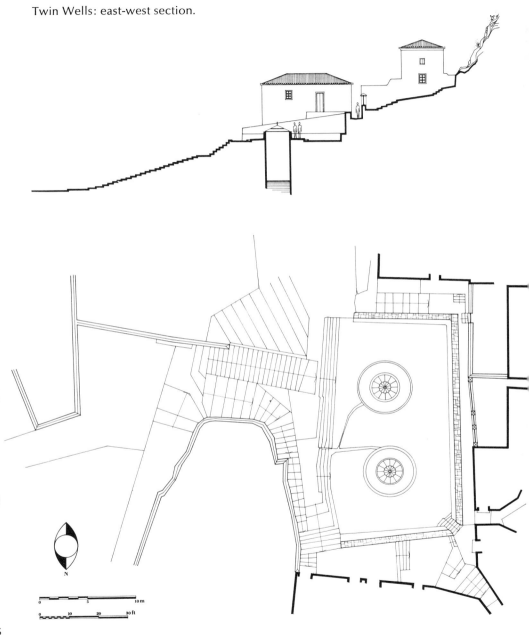

Twin Wells: east-west section.

N

| 0 | | 5 | | 10 m |
| 0 | 10 | 20 | | 30 ft |

Twin Wells: plan.

77

Twin Wells seen from the heights on its west side.

Sequence of seven photographs taken in the area of the Twin Wells. Diagram on the right identifies the position from which each numbered photograph was taken.

1

2

3

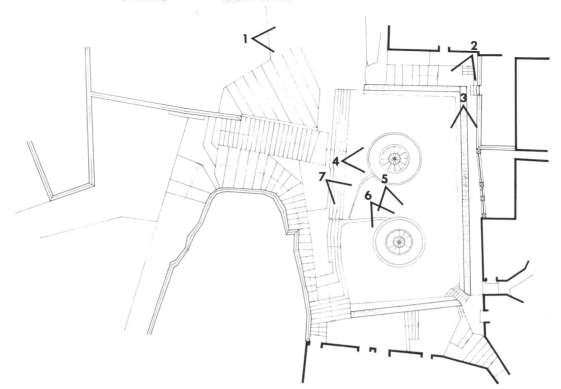

5

6

7

Typical details from *archontica*. Note the screen walls, the restrained protrusion of the eaves, and the placement of window frames in relation to the wall. Also note the window blinds which are placed on the inside of the window to make them more easily accessible. Blinds are reset very often, according to

the time of day, in response to the position of the sun, the intensity of light, and so forth. The far right photograph illustrates how the shape of the window bars allows one to lean from the window to observe activities in the street.

## VOULGARIS' HOUSE

*Archontica*, the houses of prominent families, were built within the limits of today's town and at its edges. However, the architectural character of an *archontico* was not influenced by its particular location with respect to the town. These palatial residences are distinguished from the common houses by a number of features. In size, they tower over all other structures. In form, the main house is always rectangular and approaches a cube in volume. Their architectural character is very much determined by the exposed grey stone masonry which is laid in regular coursing, and by the direct,

restrained, and unpretentious manner in which the façades are treated.

These façades are thought of as screens separating the life within the building from that outside it, and as such they are strictly two-dimensional. The roof eaves protrude very little, window frames are placed on the same plane with the masonry surface, and three-dimensional embellishment is totally lacking. The only departure from this very restrained treatment is found in the whitewashing of the window outlines, together with the relieving arches above them.

Voulgaris' house, built around the turn of the nineteenth

*Archontico* of Tombazis on the east side of the port.

81

Exterior walls of Voulgaris' house. Note the tie-rod anchors needed because of the substantial height of the masonry wall. It is also interesting to note the whitewashing band that follows the window frame and covers the area between the arch and the window, serving to identify and separate the complete window perforation from the load-bearing wall.

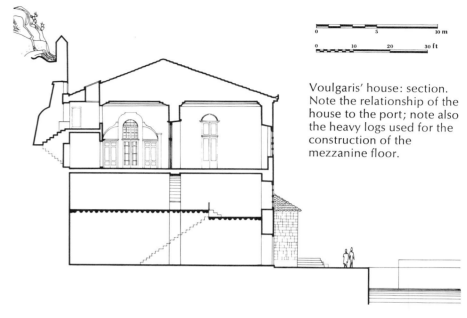

Voulgaris' house: section. Note the relationship of the house to the port; note also the heavy logs used for the construction of the mezzanine floor.

century for Frangescos Voulgaris, brother of the governor, is in many ways representative of the *archontica.* But the relationship of the house to the port and the town, achieved through the elevated courtyard, gives to this *archontico* a strong urban character unique in the whole group.

The two ends of the main-level plan of the house—the elongated part at its north end, which is the old part, and the rectangular "main" house at its south end, which is a later addition—reveal a difference in attitude in the composition of spaces. This difference in attitude is expressed by the shift from an informal composition (one room next to another) to a strictly-by-axial formal arrangement. This shift also reflects the great change through which Hydra and the owning family

passed over a period of time. Changes in the family's financial status and in their attitude toward life brought about through contact with the Western world are recorded in the house. The sophistication and formality of the new house plan point to the strong possibility that foreign builders (probably North Italian) were brought in for the construction of the *archontica.* That this house was meant to provide for more complex social life than that provided for in the traditional Hydriot house is reflected by the mezzanine orchestra balcony shown in the section drawing.

Despite this substantial change, however, the traditional spatial sequence leading to the house has been retained. The first penetration from the public street occurs at the foot of

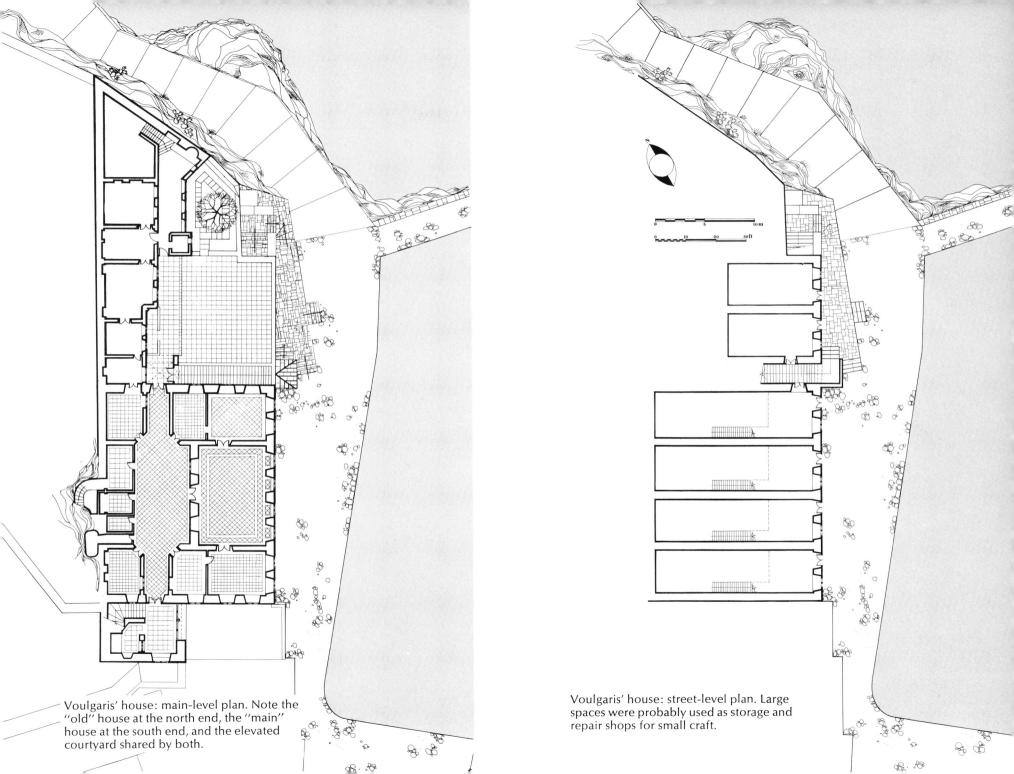

Voulgaris' house: main-level plan. Note the "old" house at the north end, the "main" house at the south end, and the elevated courtyard shared by both.

Voulgaris' house: street-level plan. Large spaces were probably used as storage and repair shops for small craft.

0      5      10 m

0    10    20    30 ft

Voulgaris' house as seen from the east side of the port.

Voulgaris' house: entry to the house from the street (far left); steps leading to the courtyard (left); entry to the "main" house as seen from the courtyard (right); and reception room of the house (far right). Note the orchestra balcony opening at the upper right of this photograph.

the entry stairs. At the top of these stairs one finds oneself in the private, uncovered space—here somewhat formalized —and then finally in the main house itself.

It is very possible that the desire to match the floor level of the old part of the house brought the main level of the new house at a considerable height above the quay and created the high ceilinged spaces below it. The size of the front openings at the street level would indicate that these spaces were probably used as storage and repair shops for small craft.

The two-level mezzanine floor built with heavy logs in shipbuilding fashion, as well as the skylights over the stairs and the orchestra booth, shown a remarkably fresh and courageous attitude toward solving architectural problems. The considerable thickness of the walls (about three feet) is mainly structural, but it also insulates the house. A concern with issues of environmental control is also shown by the slanted window sides (see plans of the house) which allow a maximum amount of light with a minimum amount of exposure.

85

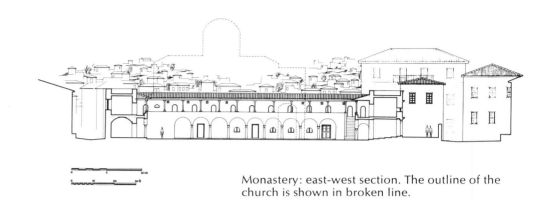

Monastery: east-west section. The outline of the church is shown in broken line.

## THE MONASTERY

The same site has been occupied by the monastery since the 1640's, but most of the present buildings were built between 1774 and 1776 to replace those destroyed by an earthquake in 1769. Some parts were added later, such as the 1870 narthex of the church. There is not much information regarding the monastery between the 1640's and 1769, but it seems certain that what the earthquake destroyed were not the original buildings.

Monasteries were established to provide for a life detached from worldly affairs. But in Hydra, the particular position of the monastery in terms of location (right in the center of the town) and in terms of importance in the historical development of the town made it an indispensable part of town life. Thus the church of the monastery was used mostly as a parish church and eventually became the cathedral, while the monastery's affairs were administered with the participation of non-clerical representatives from the town. At the same time the numerous individual donations testify to the loyalty and affection the citizens of Hydra felt for the monastery.

During the years of the Greek War of Independence, the refectory was used as a meeting room for the sea captains and town leaders planning revolutionary strategy. The same room is used today as the formal meeting room of the town council, while the immediately adjacent rooms and cells serve as the City Hall offices. Other cells house a variety of community as well as ecclesiastical offices.

Thus the building is today both the religious and the

The monastery in relation to the town and the port.

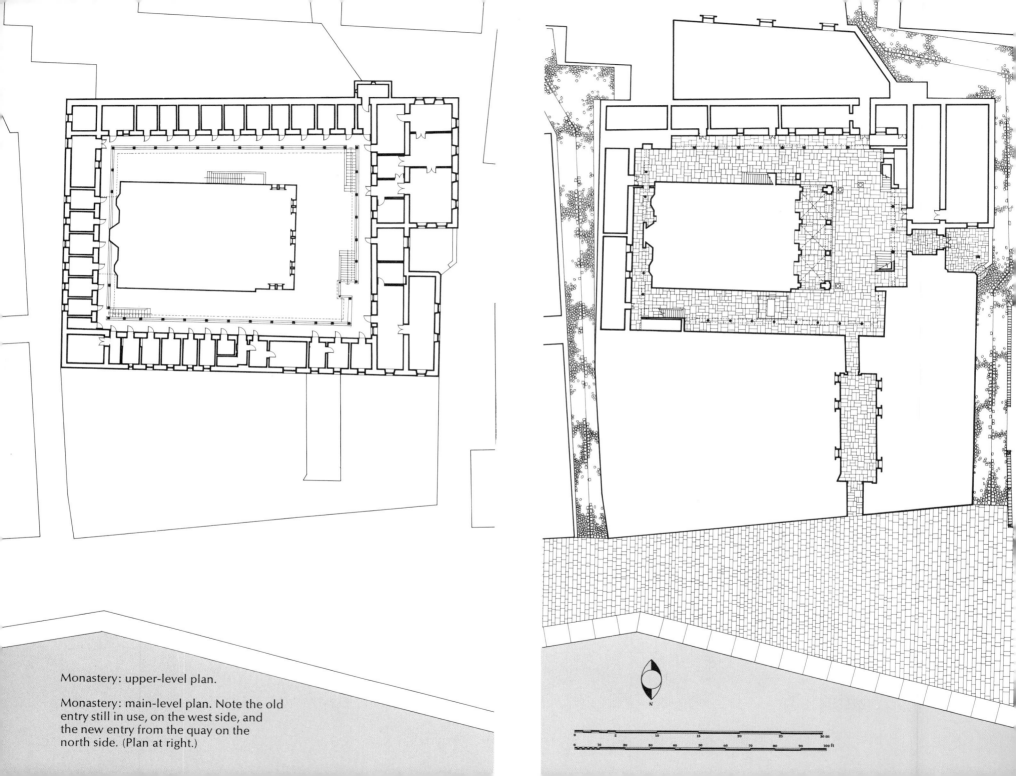

Monastery: upper-level plan.

Monastery: main-level plan. Note the old entry still in use, on the west side, and the new entry from the quay on the north side. (Plan at right.)

N

0    5    10    15    20    25        50 m

0   10   20   30   40   50   60   70   80   90   100 ft

A late eighteenth-century lithograph of the monastery by Castellan (*Lettres sur la Morée,* Paris, 1808), obviously done from memory because it contains a number of inaccuracies.

governmental center of the island. This double identity can be explained in terms of the traditional relationship between church and state in Greek history. The transformation from monastery to religious and governmental center took place gradually, its last stage beginning at the conclusion of the War of Independence when the church became the cathedral of the town.

The monastery complex is organized on the traditional pattern: a paved court on which the church stands free and which is completely enclosed on all of its four sides by two tiers of inward-looking cells. The old entry to the court on the west wall is still in use, while the newer entry through the north side of the court is an obvious concession to the uses of the quay. This new entry establishes a continuity between the various spaces of the town's civic center—a continuity which is strongly expressed by a large space–small space rhythm in this manner: quay—monastery entry—monastery court—church narthex—church proper. The longitudinal

89

Views of the courtyard of the monastery: 1. Old entry from the west side; 2. Northeast corner, with the church on the right; 3. Gallery and cells on the south side; 4. West side; 5. Flags used as decorative elements on a religious-national holiday; 6. Gallery on the east side, the church altar on the left; 7. Northwest corner and entry from the quay; 8. Southwest corner (note the houses ascending in the background).

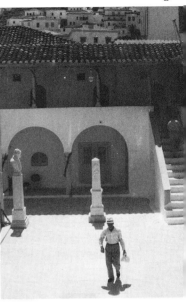

section through the monastery, and a number of related photographs, illustrate the important relationship of the court to the rest of town.

The complex has no exterior façade, since it looks inward to the court. The two-story arcade in front of the cells is a valuable architectural element elegantly executed. It can be traced back to classic and early Hellenic origins, serving as a transition space between the small and dimly lit cells and the large and brightly lit open court, effectively bridging their differences of light intensity.

The heavy masonry arches of the ground level are convincingly related to the light wood structure of the level above, and the direct and unpretentious manner in which the staircases are located and related to the arches is equally well matched by the vertical relationship of supports of the upper and lower arcades.

# SOME FINAL THOUGHTS

I said in the preface that this study would attempt to enrich our understanding of the city. *Hydra* was thought of as a document, a visual presentation of the morphological growth of a town. Certainly many more similar studies will be needed before an attempt can be made to draw any "conclusions" relevant to our own modern cities—if such a notion is justifiable at all. However, a few modest reflections on the study may be appropriate here.

We tend to explain the difficulties we experience in the formation of our environment as the result of the rapid growth of our cities. It is of interest to note that Hydra grew in a very short period of about forty years.

The economic boom which produced the town was, however, in our terms, somewhat peripheral. That boom simply meant an accumulation of cash resulting from fortuitous circumstances external to the life of the island. The social and economic aspects of life in the town remained for all practical purposes untransformed. Nothing comparable to the Industrial Revolution ever touched the island. As a result, the growth of the town followed time-honored customs and practices: the same simple materials were used, the same unwritten building codes were followed. The same concepts of spatial organization were also followed, since both the social and the technological aspects of life on the island remained unchanged.

Hydra, in our own terms again, was a small town. Undoubtedly its size, in addition to its physical characteristics, contributed in impressing the Hydriots with its perceptible form in unmistakable terms. We tend to think that form is a product of certain functions, or better stated, that form and function are interacting elements. In this context Hydra supports the notion that a powerful and dignified form can remain so even if its original functions are replaced by others.

# BIBLIOGRAPHY

Anderson, Rufus. *Observations upon the Peloponnesos and Greek Islands Made in 1829.* Boston: Crocker & Brewster, 1830.

Basileiou, Spyros (ed.). *Greek Merchant Ships 1861–1961.* Seamen's Pension Fund Centenary Edition. Athens, 1961.

Belle, Henri. *Trois Années en Grèce.* Paris: Hachette, 1881.

Berve, Helmut, and Gruben, Gottfried. *Greek Temples, Theatres and Shrines.* Photographs by Max Hirmer. New York: H. N. Abrams, 1963.

Bieber, Margarete. *The History of the Greek and Roman Theater.* 2d ed. Princeton, N. J.: Princeton University Press, 1961.

Castellan, A. L. *Lettres sur la Morée.* Paris, 1808.

Chandler, Richard. *Travels in Asia Minor and Greece: or, An Account of a Tour Made at the Expense of the Society of Dilettani.* 3d ed. London: J. Hooker, 1817.

Culver, Henry B. *The Book of Old Ships.* Garden City, N.Y.: Doubleday, Page, 1928.

Egli, Ernst. *Die neue Stadt in Landschaft und Klima: Climate and Town Districts, Consequences and Demands.* Erlenbach-Zurich: Verlag für Architektur, 1951.

Evangelides, Tryfon E. *Istoria tou epikismou tis Hydras.* Athens, 1935.

Hartley, Reverend John. *Researches in Greece and the Levant.* London, 1831.

Holland, Thomas E. *A Lecture on the Treaty Relations of Russia and Turkey from 1774 to 1853.* London: Macmillan, 1877.

Kriezis, George D. *Istoria tis nisou Hydras.* Patras, 1860.

Landström, Björn. *The Ship: An Illustrated History.* Garden City, N.Y.: Doubleday, 1961.

Lignos, Antonios. *Istoria tis nisou Hydras.* Athens, 1946.

Linton, William. *The Scenery of Greece and Its Islands.* London, 1842.

Lloyd, Christopher. *Ships and Seamen from the Vikings to the Present Day.* Cleveland: World Publishing Co., 1963.

McCandless, Byron, and Grosvenor, Gilbert. *Flags of the World.* Washington, D. C.: National Geographic Society, 1917.

Marriott, John A. R. *The Eastern Question: An Historical Study in European Diplomacy.* 4th ed. Oxford: Clarendon Press, 1951.

Matton, Raymond. *Hydra et la Guerre Maritime: 1821–1827.* (*Villes et Paysages de Grèce,* 2. Collection de l'Institut Français d'Athènes, 65.) Athens, 1953.

Melas, Spyros. *O Navarhos Miaoulis.* Athens, 1932.

Miaoulis, Antonios A. *Istoria tis nisou Hydras.* With comments and additions by Ant. N. Manikis. Athens, 1936.

Mitarachi, Paul J., and Ernest, Robert. "Mykonos and Patmos," *Perspecta: The Yale Architectural Journal,* VI (1960), 78–87.

Moholy-Nagy, Sibyl. *Native Genius in Anonymous Architecture.* New York: Horizon Press, 1957.

Morison, Samuel Eliot. *The Maritime History of Massachusetts, 1783–1860.* Boston: Houghton Mifflin Company, 1941.

Paparregopoulos, Constantine. *Istoria tou Ellinikou Ethnous.* Vol. VI. Athens, 1930.

Phillipson, Coleman, and Buxton, Noel. *The Question of the Bosphorus and Dardanelles.* London: Stevens and Haynes, 1917.

Phokas, Dimitris. *Karavia tou Agonos.* Athens, 1938.

Siegfried, André. *The Mediterranean.* New York: Duell, Sloane and Pearce, 1947.

Singer, Charles, *et al.* (eds.). *From the Renaissance to the Industrial Revolution: c1500 to c1750.* (*A History of Technology,* Vol. III.) Oxford: Clarendon Press, 1957.

Singer, Charles, *et al.* (eds.). *The Industrial Revolution: c1750 to c1850.* (*A History of Technology,* Vol. IV.) Oxford: Clarendon Press, 1958.

*Statistical Yearbook of Greece, 1962.* Athens: National Statistical Service of Greece, 1963.

Thucydides. *The History of the Peloponnesian War.* Translated by Richard Crawley. (Everyman's Library, Classical.) London: Dent; New York: Dutton, 1936.

Waddington, George. *A Visit to Greece in 1823 and 1824.* 2d ed. London: J. Murray, 1825.

Zevi, Bruno. *Biaggio Rossetti, Architetto ferrarese: il Primo Urbanista Moderno Europeo.* Turin: Giulio Einaudi, 1960.